George John Romanes and the struggle for Darwin's mantle

George John Romanes
(Photograph by Elliott & Fry, frontispiece of Romanes, 1896)

Roberto de Andrade Martins

George John Romanes and the struggle for Darwin's mantle

Containing Romanes' 1886 article on Physiological Selection

Privatus Typus
2017

Copyright © 2017 Roberto de Andrade Martins

All rights reserved.

No part of this publication may be reproduced or transmitted in any form or by any means, electronic or mechanical, including photocopying, recording, or any information storage or retrieval system, without prior permission in writing from the author.

ISBN: 9781521700037

I cordially, however, agree with the *Times*, which says that " Mr. George Romanes appears to be the biological investigator on whom the mantle of Mr. Darwin has most conspicuously descended" (August 16, 1886). Mr. Romanes is just the person whom the late Mr. Darwin would select to carry on his work, and Mr. Darwin was just the kind of person towards whom Mr. Romanes would find himself instinctively attracted. (Butler, 1910, p. 65).

Summary

First part: Romanes' struggle 1

Introduction: Darwin's mantle 3
The young Romanes meets Darwin......................................9
Romanes' early researches: medusae and pangenesis.....................13
Animal intelligence 21
Romanes' early theoretical proposals..................................25
Stepping out of Darwin's shadow 29
Physiological selection 33
Reaction against Romanes...41
Relevant tests of physiological selection.............................45
Darwin, and after Darwin..49
An examination of Weismannism 59
Inheritance of acquired characters 65
Romanes' illness 75
Final remarks 79
References 81

Second part: Physiological selection..............................87

Introduction 89
Difficulties against Natural Selection as a Theory of the Origin of Species...91
Sterility between Species..94
Swamping Effects of Intercrossing 96
Inutility of Specific Characters......................................97
Natural Selection not a Theory of the Origin of Species..................98
Evolution of Species by Independent Variation 102
Physiological Selection, or Segregation of the Fit 104
Arguments à priori 108
Arguments à posteriori 119
Argument from Sterility between Species............................120
Argument from the Prevention of Intercrossing.....................132
Argument from the Inutility of Specific Differences 135
Argument from Divergence of Character............................138
Argument from Geographical Distribution 162

Relations between Survival of the Fittest and Segregation of the Fit.. 148
General Summary and Conclusion.. 151
Postscript 159

First part: Romanes' struggle

Introduction: Darwin's mantle

George John Romanes is little known nowadays. In the late nineteenth century he came to be regarded as the most important follower of Darwin. His topmost contribution to evolution theory was the hypothesis of Physiological Selection, a mechanism that would explain speciation without geographical isolation. This work was presented to the Linnean Society in 1886, and produced a mixed reaction. Several evolutionists (such as Alfred Russel Wallace) regarded the proposal as completely wrong. Its form of presentation implied that Darwin's claim to have explained the origin of species was wrong and that he, Romanes, was providing the correct explanation.

> This had raised a storm of criticism from the senior Darwinians (Alfred Wallace, Thomas Huxley and Joseph Hooker) and their junior surrogates (Francis Darwin, William Thiselton Dyer, E. Ray Lankester and Raphael Meldola). (Forsdyke, 2010, p. 140)

There was, however, a wide repercussion. On Monday, August 16th 1886, the *London Times* published a short review of Romanes' ideas and commented:

> Mr. George Romanes appears to be the biological investigator upon whom in England the mantle of Mr. Darwin has most conspicuously descended. During many years he frequently and exhaustively discussed the whole philosophy of evolution with the distinguished author of "The Origin of Species," and thus he is in the best position for continuing and extending his work, fortified by the latest arguments, observations, and admissions of that singularly candid mind. Mr. Romanes has already propounded theories of mental evolution in animals and of the relation between mind and matter which demand much time and investigation for their proof or disproof [...]. He has lately read before the Linnean Society a remarkable paper just published, extending to 75 pages and entitled "Physiological Selection: an additional suggestion on the Origin of Species," which, if it be generally accepted, constitutes the most important addition made to the theory of evolution since the publication of "The Origin of Species." (Anon., 1886, p. 8; cf. Forsdyke, 2001, pp. 221-222; Slotten, 2012, p. 404)

The *Times* review infuriated Wallace. "As the greatest living exponent of the theory of natural selection in its pure form, Wallace felt that he was the only man who could come to the theory's defense" (Slotten, 2012, p. 404). On 28 August 1886, in a letter to Raphael Meldola, he wrote: "Romanes poses as the successor of Darwin. This sh[oul]d be stopped before the press & the public finally adopt him as such, & for this reason I wrote my paper" (Raby, 2002, p. 236).[1] Meldola had already published a criticism of Romanes' theory in *Nature* (Meldola, 1886). A few days later, Wallace's paper appeared in the *Fortnightly Review* (Wallace, 1886).

Although many outstanding researchers of the time thought that the reviewer of *The Times* had incorrectly assigned Darwin's mantle to Romanes, the expression and the attribution became well known. It was sometimes used by Romanes' friends – for instance, in the memorial note published by *The Monist* when Romanes passed away: "George John Romanes, the great English naturalist, upon whom, it was said, the mantle of Darwin fell, died on May 23, in the prime of manhood. We are deeply moved at the sad news, and feel his death as our personal loss [...]" (Anon., 1894, p. 482)

More often, however, the association of mantle's Darwin with Romanes was mentioned by his critics.

> Professor Romanes is, I believe, a most eminent biologist, and the mantle of Darwin is said to have fallen on his shoulders. Far be it from me to venture to criticise his biological facts. But we see in his case how dangerous it is for a man who can claim to speak with authority on his own special subject, to venture to speak authoritatively on subjects not his own. (Müller, 1891, p. 582)

Samuel Butler, the critic of natural selection, who also became involved in a controversy with Romanes, referred four times to Darwin's mantle in a book he first published in 1886, shortly after the publication of the theory of physiological selection and the *Times* review: "The late Mr. Darwin himself – whose mantle seems to have

---

[1] Wallace's letters are fully available at the Wallace Letters Online website. This letter from Wallace to Meldola (letter WCP4496) can be found at <http://www.nhm.ac.uk/research-curation/scientific-resources/collections/library-collections/wallace-letters-online/4496/4804/T/details.html>. Those sentences quoted above, that appear at the end of the letter, were omitted from the book *Alfred Russel Wallace – letters and reminiscences* that, nevertheless, reproduces the rest of the document (Marchant, 1916, vol. 2, pp. 36-38).

fallen more especially and particularly on Mr. Romanes – could not contradict himself more hopelessly than Mr. Romanes often does" (Butler, 1910, p. 54); "Fortunately Mr. Romanes is not Mr. Darwin, and though he has certainly got Mr. Darwin's mantle, and got it very much too, it will not on Mr. Romanes' shoulders hide a good deal that people were not going to observe too closely while Mr. Darwin wore it" (Butler, 1910, p. 61).

Nowadays, Romanes is seldom described as the heir of Darwin's mantle, with the curious exception of the Cambridge University Press reprints of his books on evolutionary psychology (*Mental evolution in animals*, and *Mental evolution in man*), which are advertised with this comment: "George John Romanes (1848–94) was considered by *The Times* to be 'the biological investigator upon whom in England the mantle of Mr. Darwin has most conspicuously descended'".[2]

Fair or unfair, the symbolic attribution of Darwin's mantle to Romanes is taken here as a starting point of a historical analysis of the career of this researcher. The subject of this book is Romanes' association with Darwin and his theory, both before and after the death of the master in 1882; and Romanes' professional strategy, likely intended to attain the status of Darwin's intellectual heir.

The young researcher established a strong collaboration with Darwin and, among other things, devoted a lot of work attempting to find experimental evidence for the latter's hypothesis of pangenesis, which was supposed to explain the inheritance of acquired characters. During Darwin's life, Romanes remained under his shadow, being one among many of his associates and supporters of evolution. During this period of eight years he had frequent meetings with the unquestioned leader of evolution theory, benefiting from his experience, ideas and making use of some of his unpublished works – for instance, Darwin's manuscript about animal instincts. George Romanes supported the theory of evolution and tried to improve it, providing suggestions concerning some of its many difficulties at the time. Strictly speaking, a follower of Darwin would only attempt to develop and to diffuse his ideas, to apply them to new cases, to obtain

---

[2] See the book descriptions available at the Cambridge University Press website:
<https://www.cambridge.org/core/books/mental-evolution-in-animals/78D5893C115A437DAEFDCB3572B40E4F#fndtn-information> and
<https://www.cambridge.org/core/books/mental-evolution-in-man/0E8D5D55AF589F42CB2425429A745F81#fndtn-information>.

new evidence for the theory of evolution and natural selection, and to answer to problems and objections against Darwin's theory. That was the initial role played by the young researcher.

After Darwin's death, the situation changed. Romanes was now 34 years old. Although he was already a Fellow of the Royal Society (since 1879), he had no position at any university. His mentor gone, he had to establish a position for himself. This his did in 1886 by claiming that the theory of natural selection had unsurmountable problems and that the origin of species could only be explained by his own additional proposal – the hypothesis (or theory) of physiological selection. Romanes' original contribution was accompanied by a criticism of Darwin's work. His new attitude might be regarded as an effort to step out of Darwin's shadow and to exhibit his own brightness. If that move were successful, he would become the foremost evolutionist, after Darwin – as the anonymous author of the *Times* note correctly pointed out.

However, after Darwin's passing, not only Romanes but other evolutionists had a similar goal. Wallace, who had arrived to the theory of natural selection independently of Darwin, was a strong candidate for the master's mantle. Herbert Spencer, Thomas Huxley and other eminent men of Darwin's circle could also claim the position of leadership. The new generation also had other strong candidates, such as August Weismann.

Neither Romanes nor the other possible heirs of Darwin's mantle accepted the old man's ideas unconditionally. They had different views concerning gradualism, the sufficiency of natural selection, heredity, the relevance of the inheritance of characters acquired by use and disuse, and several other points. Each one attempted to correct and to complement Darwin's theory by introducing new concepts and hypotheses, sometimes rejecting and criticizing several features of the original proposal. In this situation, there was a strong competition for acquiring the status of topmost evolutionist of the late nineteenth century. Each one tried to promote his own contribution and to undermine the work of other Darwinians who were fighting for that position. Romanes was no exception and he participated in several bitter disputes.

From 1886 onward, Romanes' professional career thrived. He was an invited lecturer at University of Edinburgh from 1886 to 1890, and he obtained a position at the University of Oxford in 1890. However, his health was not very good and he died in 1894, when he was only 46 years old.

This book has two parts. The first one contains a brief scientific biography of George John Romanes, with special emphasis on his connection with Darwin and evolution theory. Due to this specific approach, the biographical account will not deal with Romanes' poetry, religious interests and other features of his life that have little connection with the theory of evolution.

Information concerning Romanes' struggle with religion and faith can be found in the recente publication of his letters (Schwartz, 2010), and in the analysis of his "Memorial poem" in honour of Darwin (Pleins, 2014). Most of the current book was written before Joel Schwartz's publication of George John Romanes' letters (Schwartz, 2010). I have intensely used the century-old edition of Romanes' life and letters by his wife, Ethel (Romanes, 1896). It is known that Ethel chose the letters she published, and edited them, so as to convey the impression that her husband had undergone a religious convertion at the end of his life. This subject is not a concern of this book, however.

The discussion of the validity or otherwise of Romanes' theory is also outside the scope of the present study. In recent years, Donald Forsdyke has claimed that new bioinformatic analyses of the DNA sequence data that emerged from various genome projects in the 1990s suggest that we may now be able to support Romanes' theory of physiological selection in chemical terms (Forsdyke, 2001; Forsdyke, 2006). Some critics suggest that Forsdyke's account of Romanes' ideas is historically flawed (Lynch, 2004). I will not enter this discussion.

The second part of the book contains Romanes' 1886 article on physiological selection, complemented by several footnotes providing additional information and pointing out some particularly strong or weak points of the paper. I am grateful to the Linnean Society for permission to reproduce the full text of the article.

A first version of the present work was produced in 1999, and it was presented at the Meeting of the International Society for the History, Philosophy and Social Studies of Biology (ISHPSSB), in Oaxaca, México. A short paper in Portuguese was published several years ago (Martins, 2006).

I am grateful to the Brazilian National Council for Scientific and Technological Development (CNPq) and to the São Paulo State

Research Foundation (FAPESP) for supporting this research during several periods of its elaboration.

The young Romanes meets Darwin

The early scientific career of the Canadian born George John Romanes (1848-1894) flourished under Charles Darwin's protection. In 1870, while he was a student at Cambridge, Romanes started physiological research under Michael Foster's supervision and soon began to study Darwin's works (Lesch, 1970). In 1873, he discussed an evolutionary issue in a letter to *Nature* that called the attention of Darwin himself (Romanes, 1873). The old man wrote a kind letter to the young student, starting a relationship that was to last for one decade. In the next year, Darwin invited Romanes to meet him. There followed a friendship and collaboration between the two men. According to Romanes' wife Ethel:

> From that time began an unbroken friendship, marked on one side by absolute worship, reverence, and affection, on the other by an almost fatherly kindness and a wonderful interest in the younger man's work and in his career. (Romanes, 1896, p. 14)

Of course, their relationship was asymmetric. When they first met, Romanes was 26 years old and had published no relevant scientific contribution. Darwin, who was 65, had already published his main evolutionary works (*Origin of species, Variation of animals and plants under domestication, Descent of man*). Why did Darwin take a special interest on Romanes?

Joel Schwartz has already analyzed some features of the relationship between Darwin and Romanes (Schwartz, 1995). According to him, at the time when Romanes published that letter in *Nature*, Darwin was in need of a "strong advocate". New views on evolution (especially neo-Lamarckism) were spreading all over the world. Even followers of Darwinism, such as Alfred Russell Wallace, supported interpretations that were widely different from Darwin's own ideas[3].

---

[3] Wallace did not accept Darwin's theory of sexual selection. He held rigidly to the theory of natural selection, without allowing any other causes for organic evolution. Besides that, he claimed that natural causes were unable to explain the origin of the human mental ability (Wallace 1869).

Since the publication of the *Origin of species*, Darwin had attempted to gather a group of key persons who would support his theory. In a letter to Huxley, he wrote: "If we can once make a compact set of believers we shall in time conquer" (Darwin to Huxley, 27/Nov./59, in: Darwin, 1887, vol. 2, p. 282). This initial group included (besides Darwin and Wallace): Thomas Huxley, Joseph Dalton Hooker, Charles Lyell and a few others (Bowler, 1990, p. 131; Bowler, 1989, p. 193).

In the main, Darwin's theory was successful, and "By the 1880s, a well-entrenched school of Darwinism had become a dominant feature of the scientific establishment" (Bowler, 1989, p. 194). However, there was not a complete scientific agreement within the group. "The Darwinians formed a tightly-knit group held together by personal loyalties and commitment to a particular ideology" (Bowler, 1990, p. 150).

> Within these principles, the chief Darwinists themselves disagreed considerably over details. Darwin accepted a small element of Lamarckism; T. H. Huxley was a saltationist; while Wallace even advocated divine intervention in the evolution of man. This flexibility helped to disarm the critics, because objections to natural selection could be sidestepped by appealing to the possibility of supplementary mechanisms. At the same time, the Darwinists never fought openly among themselves. They agreed to differ in the hope that future research would solve their problems and thus were able to present a united front to the world, confident that their basic ideas were sound. (Bowler, 1989, p. 195)

Thomas Huxley always tried to support Darwin's theory, but as a matter of fact Darwin was not altogether happy with Huxley's interpretation of natural selection[4]. It seems that Huxley was not highly committed to the details of Darwin's theory (Bowler, 1990, pp. 142-145). Besides all that, in the early 1870's Darwin was fighting new battles.

---

[4] "So Huxley had reservations about the role of natural selection even though he praised Darwin and sprang to his defense. Darwin, in his turn, had reservations about Huxley's understanding of natural selection. After hearing Huxley speak on evolution in 1860, he said that 'as an exposition of the doctrine the lecture seems to me an entire failure' and added: 'He gave no just idea of Natural Selection'." (Young, 1962, p. 151).

In 1868 he had published the first edition of *The variation of animals and plants under domestication*, where he proposed his hypothesis of pangenesis to account for hereditary phenomena. Besides explaining many phenomena widely accepted by everyone, the hypothesis of pangenesis provided a theoretical basis for the inheritance of characters acquired by use or disuse[5].

This hypothesis was very dear to Darwin. It has been argued sometimes that Charles Darwin only invented the hypothesis of pangenesis as an answer to Fleeming Jenkin's criticisms published in June 1867. However, Peter Vorzimmer has convincingly argued that the proposal of pangenesis was independent of Jenkin's paper (Vorzimmer, 1963, p. 386)[6].

Pangenesis was attacked by many authors, including Darwin's cousin Francis Galton, who in 1871 published the result of experiments providing evidence against that hypothesis (Galton, 1871; see also Darwin's reply: Darwin, 1871). Charles Darwin really needed someone who clearly understood and agreed with his theory and who could defend him. As we shall see, Romanes endeavored to fill this gap.

From 1875 to Darwin's death (1882), Romanes was his close disciple and assistant. As will be shown below, he endeavored to improve, extend and defend Darwin's theory. He always asked for Darwin's help and advice, and they seldom disagreed with each other. After Darwin's passing, however, Romanes adopted a new attitude. It seems that he attempted to fill the vacant place and to become the leader of Darwinian [7] evolutionary research. According to the reconstruction of his strategy shown here, he tried to weaken the position of other candidates to Darwin's heritage. He also built for himself a more appropriate profile, with the proposal of a

---

[5] Darwin always accepted the "Lamarkian" concept of use-disuse and inheritance of acquired characters. This principle is explicitly used in the *Origin of species*, and the *Variation* provided detailed evidence for it.

[6] One relevant piece of evidence that Vorzimmer did not use was Darwin's *Diary*, where it was clearly recorded that the chapter on pangenesis of *The variation of animals and plants under domestication* was finished on the 21st November 1866 (Darwin, 1887, vol. 3, p. 42).

[7] Here I adopt a very broad characterization of 'Darwinians' to include all those who claimed that Darwin's theory was the best available, and who regarded themselves as followers of Darwin.

complementary theory ("physiological selection") that, if accepted, would place Romanes in a top position within evolutionary research.

Romanes' early researches: medusae and pangenesis

Romanes' scientific interests varied widely during his lifetime. Before Darwin's death, his main contributions to evolution theory were:
1. A detailed study of the mechanism of motion and of the nervous system of lower invertebrates (jellyfishes, starfishes, sea urchins) and the evolutionary significance of those findings.
2. An attempt to provide experimental evidence for Darwin's hypothesis of pangenesis.
3. A comparative study of animal and human intelligence, attempting to show that the mental evolution of animals led smoothly to the development of men's mental power.

He also presented minor contributions on other specific points, such as the reduction of useless organs. Moreover, Romanes was a highly successful lecturer, and produced popular but fairly rigorous presentations of Darwin's ideas.

His earliest researches, which began under Foster's supervision (1873), dealt with the physiology of jellyfishes. He studied the motion of medusae, presenting his first results as a M. A. dissertation (1874). After leaving Cambridge, the twenty six years old Romanes moved to London, where he continued his researches on medusae under William Sharpey and John Burdon-Sanderson at the University College. His family was wealthy, and he did not need any job – he devoted himself to scientific research just because he enjoyed it. For many years he maintained his own private laboratory in Dunskaith, where he spent the summers studying sea life (Romanes, 1896, p. 14). This was Romanes' profile when he first met Darwin: he was an experimental physiologist.

It seems that Darwin was strongly impressed by Romanes. They talked about pangenesis, and agreed that Romanes could attempt to find experimental evidence for this hypothesis.

Darwin had strong doubts that his hypothesis of pangenesis would be accepted, but nevertheless he entertained at the same time a hope that it would be "proved" by experiment in the future and would then be accepted. In his *Autobiography*, Darwin remarked:

> Towards the end of the work [*Variation of animals and plants under domestication*] I give my well-abused hypothesis of Pangenesis. An unverified hypothesis is of little or no value. But if any one should hereafter be led to make observations by which some such hypothesis could be established, I shall have done good service, as an astonishing number of isolated facts can thus be connected together and rendered intelligible. (Darwin, 1948, p. 130)

In a letter to Hooker (February 23, 1868), Darwin wrote:

> You will think me very self-sufficient, when I declare that I feel *sure* if Pangenesis is now still born it will, thank God, at some future time reappear, begotten by some other father, and christened by some other name.
>
> Have you ever met with any tangible and clear view of what takes place in generation, whether by seeds or buds, or how a long-lost character can possibly reappear; or how the male element can possibly affect the mother plant, or the mother animal, so that her future progeny are affected? Now all these points and many others are connected together, whether truly or falsely is another question, by Pangenesis. You see I die hard, and stick up for my poor child. (Darwin, 1887, vol. 3, p. 78)

This is an instance of the critique suffered by pangenesis:

> Pangenesis has not the advantages of Natural Selection, and cannot therefore hope for so ready an acceptance. It has the disadvantage of not being readily grasped, nor easily brought into confrontation with facts. It has the still greater disadvantage of being hypothetical throughout: not being one supposition put forward to harmonise a series of facts, but a series of suppositions, every one of which needs proof. (Lewes, 1868, p. 507)

Two years later, after the hypothesis had received a lot of criticism, Darwin wrote to Edwin Lankester (March 15, 1870): "I was pleased to see you refer to my much despised child, 'Pangenesis', who I think will someday, under some better nurse, turn out a fine stripling" (Darwin, 1887, vol. 3, p. 120). Was Darwin trying to draw Lankester to help him? If that was his aim, he was not successful.

Taking into account those precedents, it is obvious that Darwin was eager to obtain Romanes' help. The main line of research he proposed involved an attempt to produce graft hybrids[8]. In the beginning of 1875, Romanes was already intensively working on experimental pangenesis, as shown by his letters to Darwin (Romanes, 1896, p. 21). All training Romanes had received was in invertebrate physiology. He had no training whatsoever in botanical experiments. However, he tried hard to obtain significant results, and Darwin had great expectations concerning those trials:

> I have been much interested by your letter, and am truly delighted at the prospect of success. Such energy as yours is almost sure to command victory. The world will be much more influenced by experiments on animals than on plants. But in any case I think a large number of successful results will be necessary to convince physiologists[9]. It is rash to be sanguine, but it will be splendid if you succeed. (Darwin to Romanes, July 18, 1875, in: Romanes, 1896, p. 33)

From the wording of Darwin's letters it is possible to perceive that he had no doubts about pangenesis and did not intend to *check* it. His aim was to *convince* others that it was a nice hypothesis. At this time, he was preparing the second edition of *The variation of animals and plants under domestication* (Darwin to Romanes, 12/July/75, in: Romanes, 1896, p. 40), and he would be delighted if he were able to provide positive evidence for pangenesis.

Besides doing botanical experiments, Romanes attempted to graft animal organs and tissues: "Eventually the passing of the Vivisection Act caused me to abandon the whole research as far as animals were concerned" (Romanes, 1892-1897, vol. 2, p. 144). Romanes, with the help of Edward Schäfer, also repeated Galton's blood transfusion experiments with rabbits, in the hope of obtaining positive results, but no effect was observed (Romanes, 1892-1897, vol. 2, pp. 145-146).

Through the influence of Darwin, Romanes soon became personally acquainted with many influential people: Thomas Huxley,

---

[8] According to the hypothesis of pangenesis, when two plants are grafted together, there should occur an interchange of "gemules" between them. Those gemules should affect the reproductive organs of the plants, and lead to the production of hybrids that could be replicated by sexual reproduction.

[9] Darwin mentioned more than once the difficulty of convincing physiologists about the value of pangenesis (see Darwin to Romanes, 12/July/1875, in: Romanes, 1896, p. 40). As Romanes was working in the physiology laboratory of Sharpey and Burdon-Sanderson and was still an associate of Foster, it is likely that he suffered some pressure from those colleagues *against* his graft experiments.

Herbert Spencer, Joseph Dalton Hooker, Francis Galton, etc.[10] In 1875 Darwin decided to propose Romanes for the Linnean Society, with the support of Huxley and Hooker (Darwin to Romanes, 24/Sept./75, in: Romanes, 1896, p. 35). Up to that time, Romanes had published no relevant scientific paper – only small notes in *Nature*. As Romanes himself told Darwin, "I am an M. A. and a fellow of the Philosophical Society of Cambridge, but otherwise I am nothing, nor have I any publication worth alluding to" (Romanes to Darwin, September 29, 1875, in: Romanes, 1896, p. 33). Of course, Darwin thought that Romanes was a promising young researcher, and wanted to please him and to lift him to a higher status.

Parallel to his involvement with pangenesis, Romanes kept working on medusae. In 1875 Romanes submitted his first paper on this subject to the Royal Society. It was published in the next year (Romanes, 1876).

For several years, Romanes studied the peculiar nervous system of jellyfishes, the sense of smell in echinodermata and other similar organisms [11]. Those investigations were relevant for the understanding of the evolution of animal intelligence among lower invertebrates[12]. His results were deemed relevant, but there was nothing revolutionary or extraordinary in those early researches.

At this time there was a public opposition against vivisection, and that was the main reason why many researchers joined to create the *Physiological Society* in 1876. Romanes (together with Gerald Yeo) was its first secretary (Romanes, 1896, p. 67). In that same year, for the first time, Romanes took part of the Annual Meeting of the *British Association for the Advancement of Science*.

At the same time, between 1875 and 1881, under Darwin's stimulation and guidance, Romanes undertook a series of experiments

---

[10] According to Schwartz, "Romanes eagerly grasped Darwin's hand of friendship. He was keenly aware that Darwin could assist his career by providing him with a much wider access to other members of the scientific community and could help him achieve greater recognition with the scientific public" (Schwartz, 1995, p. 286).

[11] It seems that Romanes began to investigate starfishes just because sometimes he could not find jellyfishes to study: "On the days when I could get no jelly-fish I took to starfish" (Romanes to Darwin, 11/Aug./77, in: Romanes, 1896, p. 61).

[12] This line of research culminated with the publication, in 1885, of his book *Jelly-fish, star-fish, and sea urchins* (1885).

intended to provide a foundation for the hypothesis of pangenesis[13]. In 1876, Darwin wrote to Romanes:

> Dear Romanes,
> As you are interested in Pangenesis, and will some day, I hope, convert an 'airy nothing' into a substantial theory, therefore I send by this post an essay by Häckel attacking 'Pan.', and substituting a molecular hypothesis. (Darwin to Romanes, undated letter [1876], in: Romanes, 1896, p. 51)

His research on medusae was going on pretty well, and gave him his first scientific papers (Romanes, 1876, 1877, 1880). At the same time, he continued to work on experimental pangenesis, with no relevant result. Why didn't he give up the unsuccessful work, and devote himself entirely to his physiological research on jellyfishes? It seems that Romanes wanted to collaborate with Darwin, and was very anxious to please him[14].

Romanes kept Darwin fully informed about the progress (and failures) of his grafting experiments. From time to time, he excused himself for dealing with other research subjects: "As you have heard about the Medusae, I fear you will infer that they must have diverted my attention from Pangenesis; but although it is true that they have consumed a great deal of time and energy, I have done my best to keep Pangenesis in the foreground" (Romanes to Darwin, 14/July/75, in: Romanes, 1896, p. 41). Again, in 1876 Romanes wrote to Darwin:

> I have an idea that you are afraid I am neglecting Pangenesis for Medusae. If so, I should like to assure you that such is not the case. Last year I gave more time to the former than to the latter inquiry; and although the results proved very disproportionate, this was only due to the fact that the one line of work was more difficult than the other. [...] I confess, however, that but for personal reasons I should have postponed Pangenesis and worked the Medusae right through in one year. There is a glitter about immediate results which is very alluring. (Romanes to Darwin, Romanes, 1896, pp. 48-49)

---

[13] The experiments never succeeded, and no publication resulted from this line of research.

[14] Darwin kept stimulating Romanes to find evidences favorable to pangenesis. See Darwin's letters in: Romanes, 1896, letter of 24/Sept./75, p. 35; letter of 12/July/75, p. 40; undated letter [1876], p. 49; undated letter [1876], p. 51; undated letter [Nov. 1877], p. 69; letter of 26/Mar./81, p. 113.

Graft experiments continued to be unsuccessful. In 1877, Darwin wrote to Romanes: "I am very sorry to hear about the failures in the graft experiments, and not from your own fault or ill-luck" (Darwin, 1903, vol. 1, p. 370). In this letter, Darwin was concerned that Romanes could give up the experiments, and even offered to help: "I cannot conceive why I have not offered my garden for your experiments. I would attend to the plants, as far as mere care goes, with pleasure; but Down is an awkward place to reach".

Romanes accepted Darwin's offer and asked him to keep some onions at Down, to avoid contamination. Again, the experiment did not succeed. He wrote to Darwin: "I am sorry to hear about the onions, and can only quote the beatitude which is particularly applicable to a worker in science, Blessed is he that expected nothing, for he shall not be disappointed. But I am still more sorry to hear of your feeling knocked up" (Romanes to Darwin 17/Aug./78, in: Romanes, 1896, pp. 75-76).

In the period from 1879 to 1881, Romanes' involvement with pangenesis decreased[15], but he always returned to the subject. In the beginning of 1881, Darwin was still stimulating Romanes to think about pangenesis, telling him about sugar cane graft-hybrids produced in Brazil (Darwin, 1903, vol. 1 p. 389-390). In March 1881 Romanes was consulting Darwin concerning new kinds of experiments he wanted to try (Romanes, 1896, p. 112). Darwin replied: "You are very plucky about Pangenesis, and I much with that you could have any success" (Darwin to Romanes, 26/Mar./81, in: Romanes, 1896, p. 113).

Many years later, Romanes clearly acknowledged to Edward Poulton, who was his adversary, that the experiments attempting to confirm pangenesis had never succeeded:

> Although I spent more time and trouble than I like to acknowledge. (even to myself) in trying to prove Pangenesis between '73 and '80, I never obtained any positive results, and did not care to publish negative. Therefore there are no papers of mine on the subject, although I may fairly believe that no other human being has tried so many experiments upon it. (Romanes to Poulton, 11/Nov./89, in: Romanes, 1896, p. 228)

---

[15] Probably because of his involvement with graft experiments, Romanes was invited in 1880 to write an article on 'hybridism' for the *Encyclopaedia Britannica*, and asked for Darwin's help (Romanes, 1896, p. 104).

During those years, Romanes' researches on medusae were as successful as he could possibly expect. In 1879 the 31 years old physiologist was elected a Fellow of the Royal Society (Romanes, 1896, p. 93). Up to this time, he had published only two relevant physiological investigations on Medusae in the *Philosophical Transactions of the Royal Society*. Of course, Darwin's support was instrumental in Romanes' election[16].

---

[16] In 1877 Darwin had already recommended Romanes for membership in the Royal Society (Schwartz, 1995, p. 295).

Animal intelligence

Romanes' early success in the study of lower invertebrates gave him some scientific visibility, but his results only interested the specialist. However, he soon began to expand his interest to embrace the study of intelligence and behavior of all kinds of animals, adopting an evolutionary outlook.

In 1878 he began work for a book on this subject, and delivered a lecture on animal intelligence at the *British Association* meeting (Romanes, 1896, p. 73). Darwin enjoyed Romanes' lecture, and stimulated this new line of research:

> I should like to read whole chapters on this one head, and others on the minds of the higher idiots. Nothing can be better, as it seems to me, than your several lines or sources of evidence, and the manner in which you have arranged the whole subject. Your book will assuredly be worth years of hard labour, and stick to your subject. By the way, I was pleased at your discussing the selection of varying instincts or mental tendencies, for I have often been disappointed by no one ever having noticed this notion. (Darwin to Romanes, 20/Aug./78, in: Romanes, 1896, p. 77)

In the same letter, Darwin suggested that Romanes should keep a monkey at home, to observe and describe its intelligence. Towards the end of 1880 Romanes obtained a monkey (Romanes, 1896, p. 110) and convinced his sister, Charlotte, to take care of the animal for several months. He described his observations in *Animal intelligence*[17].

Romanes began to dedicate more and more attention to compared psychology, devoting less time to physiological researches (Romanes to Darwin, 29/Aug./78, in: Romanes, 1896, pp. 79-80). In 1880 he was still doing some work on echinodermata with his friend James Cossar Ewart (Romanes, 1896, pp. 104, 109), and his last piece of research on sea life was a study concerning the smelling power of anemones (Romanes, 1896, p. 97).

---

[17] See also Romanes' own account of how in 1887 he taught a zoo chimpanzee to recognize numbers from 1 to 5 (Romanes, 1896, pp. 253-259).

> While he was carrying out this important work in physiology [on *medusae*], Romanes was gathering observations and corresponding with Darwin on the subject of animal intelligence. To both Darwin and Romanes it appeared that the theory of evolution required a fundamental continuity in the spectrum of mental life, extending from the lowest organisms up to and including man. Moreover, the ascending stages of mental development should be susceptible of explanation in terms of natural causes. Romanes set himself the task of demonstrating the fact of this continuous development and of giving an account of psychological processes in the light of their probable historical origins. (Lesch, 1970, p. 518)

Darwin felt that this was a gap in evolution theory. In the closing paragraphs of *The origin of species*, he had remarked:

> In the future I see open fields for far more important researches. Psychology will be securely based on the foundation already well laid by Mr. Herbert Spencer, that of the necessary acquirement of each mental power and capacity by gradation. Much light will be thrown on the origin of man and his history. (Darwin, 1872, p. 428)

After his mains evolutionist works (*The origin of species*, *Descent of man* and *Variation of animals and plants under domestication*), Darwin did not attempt to write any other book of general import. He wrote on specific topics, such as insectivorous plants (1875), the effect of cross- and self-fertilization (1876), the movement and habits of climbing plants (1875), and earthworms (1881). He left to others the development of important complements of his work, such as the theory of mental evolution.

> Much of Darwin's later scientific work [after *Variation* and *Descent of man*] had taken him away from the great issues of the day to concentrate on small-scale topics that could be illuminated by his particular approach to evolutionism. Far from writing a great survey of the history of life on earth he chose to investigate the origin of particular adaptations in the light of his theory of natural selection. (Bowler, 1990, p. 137)

Up to 1872 (the year of publication of the 6th edition of *The origin of species*), Darwin was waiting for someone who would take the responsibility of writing down the evolution of mind. A few years later, he put his hope in Romanes' hands. It is noteworthy that Darwin handed his unpublished notes on instincts and comparative psychology to Romanes, allowing him to make free use of his manuscript[18].

> My dear Romanes
> You are quite welcome to have my longer chapter on instinct. It was abstracted for the Origin. I have never had time to work it up in a state fit for publication, and it is so much more interesting to observe than to write. It is very unlikely that I should ever find time to prepare my several long chapters for publication, as the material collected since the publication of the Origin has been so enormous. But I have sometimes thought that when incapacitated for observing, I would look over my manuscripts, and see whether any deserved publication. You are, therefore, heartily welcome to use it, and should you desire to do so at any time, inform me and it shall be sent. (Darwin to Romanes, 19/June/78, in: Romanes, 1896, p. 74)

Darwin felt that he would be unable to develop this important complement of evolution theory, and entrusted to Romanes this new burden[19]. "G. J. Romanes, who inherited the Darwinian mantle in the area of mental evolution, expounded a development system in which social activity – via the emergence of language – was the real cause of mental progress (1888)" (Bowler, 1989, p. 236).

Romanes was able to systematize the study of animal intelligence and to present evidence for a continuous evolution of mind. His method, however, would be regarded as naïve, according to contemporary standards. He collected anecdotes (use of personal observations and descriptions he obtained in books or newspapers, often by untrained observers, uncritically accepted) and attempted to interpret animal behavior using analogy with humans and introspection: the mental processes in animals should be similar to those that occur in man. His approach was later superseded by his friend Conway Lloyd Morgan, who proposed the so-called "law of parsimony": behavior must not be interpreted in terms of higher mental process when it can be explained by lower mental process.

Romanes' research on mental evolution was criticized by several authors, including St. George Jackson Mivart, and Romanes was

---

[18] Of course, Romanes acknowledged Darwin's help, and published Darwin's manuscript as an appendix to his book *Animal intelligence* (1882).

[19] Many years before, Darwin had offered Wallace his notes on man, in the hope of motivating him to write on human evolution. Wallace, however, chose to follow a different path (Schwartz, 1995, p. 307).

always ready to fight for his work: "I think it is probable that Mivart and I shall have a magazine battle some day on Mental Evolution, as I think it is better to draw him in this way before finally discussing the whole subject in my book" (Romanes to Darwin, 5/Nov./80, in: Romanes, 1896, p. 104).

The main result of those researches was a series of books: *Animal intelligence* (1882)[20], *Mental evolution in animals* (1883), and *Mental evolution in man* (1888). Of course, the last book of this series opened a conflict between Romanes and Wallace, who could never accept that the human mind had developed from the animal mind by a continuous transition (Schwartz, 1984).

Peter Bowler criticized Romanes' approach to mental evolution as being more related to Herbert Spencer's views than to Darwin's:

> In fact Romanes' account of mental evolution owed more to the philosophy of Herbert Spencer than to Darwin's biological theory. His approach was to trace out a logically plausible sequence by which the mental functions of animals with the simplest nervous system could be developed through to the human level of intelligence. [...] Although recognizing that natural selection could act on instincts, Romanes preferred Spencer's Lamarckian approach in which instincts were produced when learned habits became so deeply ingrained that they became hereditary. (Bowler, 1990, p. 193)

One should remember, however, that Darwin accepted that use-disuse and inheritance of acquired characters had a relevant role in the origin of instincts[21], and also that he clearly stated that Herbert Spencer's approach in this respect was the best available: "In the future I see open fields for far more important researches. Psychology will be securely based on the foundation already well laid by Mr. Herbert Spencer, that of the necessary acquirement of each mental power and capacity by gradation" (Darwin, 1872, p. 428).

---

[20] *Animal intelligence* is regarded as the first book on comparative psychology ever published. The very phrase "comparative psychology" was framed by Romanes.

[21] There are several points in chapter 8 of the *Origin of species* where Darwin refers to use-inheritance as a source of instincts, and in the Summary of that chapter we can find: "In many cases habit or use and disuse have probably come into play" (Darwin, 1872, p. 233).

Romanes' early theoretical proposals

Darwin's death in April 1882 was a hard blow upon Romanes and ended the first scientific period of his life. Except for the work on jellyfishes (that had been started and developed under the influence of other researchers), Romanes' early investigations were developed in Darwin's shadow. As a faithful disciple, Romanes attempted to develop and to diffuse Darwin's ideas, to apply them to new cases, to obtain new evidence for this theory and to provide answers to problems and objections against the Darwinian theory. He had replaced Huxley as Darwin's bulldog, and he was always ready to rise and fight for his master[22]. In his writings, he always exhibited an unqualified support of Darwin's theory.

Up to this time, Romanes had only made a few timid attempts to change the theory itself. In 1874 he had proposed a new explanation for the reduction of disused organs, without the assumption of inheritance of acquired characters (Romanes, 1874)[23]. Darwin was not very enthusiastic as regards Romanes' ideas (Schwartz 1995, pp. 286-287). Romanes' later correspondence brings confirmation to the view that Darwin never abandoned the hypothesis of use-inheritance, and even dissuaded Romanes to look for an alternative:

> [...] When my paper was published, and Darwin accepted the idea with enthusiasm, I put it to him in conversation whether this idea might not supersede Lamarckian principles altogether[24]. (By carefully reading between the lines of the paper itself, you will see how much this question was occupying my mind at the time, though I did not dare to challenge Lamarck's principles *in toto* without much more full inquiry.) Then it was that Darwin dissuaded me from going on to this point, on the ground that there was abundant evidence of Lamarck's principles apart from use and disuse of structures – *e.g.* instincts – and also on the ground of his theory of Pangenesis. Therefore I abandoned the matter, and still retain what

---

[22] Romanes sometimes called Darwin 'The Master' (Romanes, 1896, p. 138).

[23] Romanes' proposal was very similar to Weismann's later ideas on panmixia (Romanes 1893).

[24] Romanes referred here to his paper: Romanes, 1874.

may thus be now a prejudice against exactly the same line of thought as Darwin talked me out of in 1873[25]. (Romanes to Poulton, 11/Nov./89, in: Romanes, 1896, p. 229)

Besides being unable to accept Romanes' proposal, a few years later Darwin favored another explanation of the same phenomenon. In 1881, Wilhelm Roux published *Der Kampf der Theile*, where he proposed that there should occur a competition between the inner parts of each organism. The hypothesis was used by Roux to explain the reduction in size of useless organs (such as the eyes of cave animals). Darwin received the book and enjoyed Roux's hypothesis. He urged Romanes to write a review about that work for *Nature* (Darwin to Romanes, 16/April/81, in: Romanes, 1896, p. 115).

Of course, Romanes was not very enthusiastic about the proposal, because Roux's ideas conflicted with his own interpretation. A few months later, Darwin insisted: "I received yesterday the enclosed notice, and I send it to you, as I have thought that if you notice Dr. Roux's book in 'Nature' or elsewhere the review might possibly be of use to you" (Darwin to Romanes, 7/Aug./81, in: Romanes, 1896, p. 125). Romanes replied: "Many thanks for the notice of Roux's book. I have not yet looked at the latter, but Preyer, of Jena (who has been our guest during the Congress meeting, and who knows the author), does not think much of it" (Romanes to Darwin, 8/Aug./81, in: Romanes, 1896, pp. 125-126).

Darwin insisted: "Two of three papers by Hermann Müller have just appeared in 'Kosmos', [...]; there is also a good and laudatory review of Dr. Roux. I could lend you 'Kosmos' if you think fit" (Darwin to Romanes, 2/Sept./81, in: Romanes, 1896, p. 130). Romanes at last decided to write the review, and answered: "I have already sent in a short review of Roux's book, but should like to see about the bees in 'Kosmos'" (Romanes to Darwin, 4/Sept./81, in: Romanes, 1896, p. 131).

A second minor conflict between Romanes and Darwin arose when the young researcher first proposed his hypothesis of physiological selection[26]. The subject Romanes addressed was the origin of divergent species from a single original species, without

---

[25] The conversation must have occurred in 1874, of course.
[26] Romanes sent his first draft on this subject to Darwin on June 6, 1877 (Romanes, 1896, p. 54).

geographical isolation[27]. As other naturalists of the time, Romanes thought that the free intercrossing of the emerging varieties would prevent the rise of two (or more) different branches from a single common species[28].

Darwin had attempted to explain this possibility in *The origin of species* with the help of natural selection (Bowler, 1989, pp. 212-214) and rejected isolation as a *necessary* condition for the rise of divergent evolution. Darwin's answer to Romanes' speculations was not very encouraging (Schwartz, 1995, pp. 299-302). Romanes withdrew his suggestion and never discussed the subject again with Darwin.

It seems that Darwin regarded his own theory as essentially correct and perceived any proposal of new ideas, in attempts to solve its difficulties, as a challenge to his own ideas. Of course, Romanes' purpose at that time was not to criticize Darwin: he was attempting to improve the theory. He understood, however, that he was treading upon dangerous ground, and chose to step back.

---

[27] The necessity of geographical isolation for the production of new species had been claimed by Moritz Wagner in 1868 (Mayr, *The growth of biological thought*, p. 563). Darwin could not accept this proposal.

[28] Peter Vorzimmer discussed the evolution of Charles Darwin's thought on blending inheritance and how it was possible to conciliate the "swamping effect" of blending inheritance with natural selection (Vorzimmer, 1963).

Stepping out of Darwin's shadow

When Romanes received the news of Darwin's death, he wrote to Francis Darwin:

> Half the interest of my life seems to have gone when I cannot look forward any more to his dear voice of welcome, or to the letters that were my greatest happiness. For now there is no one to venerate, no one to work for, or to think about while working. (Romanes to Francis Darwin, 22/April/82, in: Romanes, 1896, pp. 135-136)

Those seem sincere words.

Shortly afterwards, Romanes wrote a long "Memorial poem" as a tribute for Darwin. This work remained unknown and unpublished for more than one century, and was found and printed recently (Pleins, 2014).

It is curious that Romanes always referred to Darwin's death as a crucial date, and usually counted events from that year onward, *e.g.* "[...] four years after Darwin's death [...]" (Romanes, 1892-1897, vol. 2, p. 313).

Until 1882, Romanes had in Darwin the strongest scientific guide of his life. Up to this time, his highest ambition was to help Darwin. Now, after Darwin's departure, the profile of Romanes' work underwent a profound change. He was a distinguished 34 years old scientist, with no one to guide him, and had to choose his own path.

From 1882 to his own passing (1894), Romanes' main contributions to evolution theory were:

1. He completed his former studies on compared animal and human intelligence.
2. He proposed the theory of physiological selection (1886) and attempted to find observational and experimental support for it.
3. He delivered courses and published books presenting a popular account of Darwinism.
4. He criticized and engaged into controversy with several evolutionists (especially Herbert Spencer, August Weismann and

Alfred Wallace), trying to find experimental support against Neo-Darwinism.

According to Joel Schwartz,

> The significance of Romanes's popular writing was that by moving "out of Darwin's shadow" in defending his model of evolution, he kept Darwin's name before the public and helped secure his own place in the history of science. (Schwartz, 2002, pp. 151-152)

Romanes' work on mental evolution was an outstanding achievement, and won him some prominence[29]. Had his ambition been modest, he could rest content with this work, which had filled a *desideratum* in Darwin's program. He was regarded as Darwin's worthy disciple. He remained faithful to Darwin's memory, and was occasionally summoned by Francis Darwin to defend Darwinism:

> One of these same saints has been behaving outrageously in print, and everybody is full either of jubilation or indignation at what he has been writing about Darwin and Darwinism. F. Darwin asked me to do the replying, and to-day I am returning proof of an article for the 'Contemporary Review'. (Romanes to his sister Charlotte, 18/May/88, in: Romanes, 1896, p. 194)

It seems, however, that Romanes longed for a higher *status* in the scientific world.

It is difficult, of course, to apprehend what was going on in Romanes' mind. The interpretation that will be presented here is offered as a plausible *reconstruction* of his aims and professional strategy. That is, assuming that Romanes had in view some goals (compatible with the available evidence), it is possible to understand the main steps he took after Darwin's death as ways to attain those goals. However, this reconstruction does not amount to say that Romanes consciously planned those stages as instrumental in attaining that aim.

Romanes took part in several controversies on evolution, especially in the period from 1886 onwards. The main targets of his criticism were Herbert Spencer, Alfred Wallace and August Weismann. He avoided, however, any clashes with Thomas Huxley.

---

[29] Many historians of Psychology mention Romanes' work, but they always emphasize that his work was soon superseded.

Sometimes he referred to Huxley as one of the "highest authorities on the theory of natural selection", on a par with Darwin (Romanes, 1892-1897, vol. 2, p. 307). However, as Huxley did once criticize Romanes' views, he did reply, but his answer was of a most respectful kind (Romanes, 1892-1897, vol. 2, pp. 307-310).

> It would be quite absurd to deny that Mr. Romanes liked a fair and free fight, and there was a good deal of scientific controversy, but he was absolutely incapable of anything but fairness, and never imported into private life any quarrel in print. He had plenty of stiff fights, chiefly with Mr. Thielson-Dyer, Professor Lankester, and Mr. Wallace, but the first two were always his friends, and with the latter he had a very slight acquaintance. (Romanes, 1896, p. 93)

It is remarkable that Romanes could keep good personal exchange with several of the scientists he criticized. After a hot debate with Poulton at the 1889 British Association meeting, he was able to write a letter to his adversary in the following terms:

> My dear Poulton
> I am very glad to receive your long and friendly letter; because, although I have the Ishmael-like reputation of finding my hand against every man, and every man's against mine, my blastogenetic endowments are really of the peaceful order. (Romanes to Poulton, Sept./89, in: Romanes, 1896, p. 203)

In Romanes' biography written by his wife Ethel there is scarce information on his scientific undertakings between 1882 and 1886. Most of his time was probably taken by the preparation of the series of books on mental evolution. *Animal intelligence* had already appeared in 1881, before Darwin's passing. In 1883, Romanes published *Mental evolution in animals*, and then he probably kept busy working on *Jelly-fish, star-fish, and sea urchins* (published in 1885) and *Mental evolution in man* (1888). Between the two later books, however, he diverted his attention to something completely new, different from all his former contributions: the theory of physiological selection.

Physiological selection

In May 1886 Romanes presented a paper offering what he regarded as his most important contribution to evolutionary thought: the theory of physiological selection. He chose to communicate his ideas at the same place where Darwin and Wallace had presented their first papers on natural selection: the Linnean Society.

Shortly before the presentation of his article to the Linnean Society, Romanes sent letters to several scientists, inviting them to attend the meeting and announcing the aim of his contribution. This is the content of his letter to Raphael Meldola[30]:

> May 5th '86
> My dear Sir,
> I hope you may find it convenient to attend the next meeting of the Linnean Society, which takes place tomorrow at 8 o'clock. I am to read a paper on a new theory upon the origin of species, and should like to know what you think of it.
> To me it appears a theory of considerable importance, but on this account I want to expose it to the best criticism.
> G. J. Romanes

Notice that Romanes did not announce his work as "a contribution to Darwin's theory on the origin of species", or "a complement to the theory of natural selection", but as a *new theory upon the origin of species*. Nobody – except his closest friends – could know what he was going to present. Hence, in the night of the 6th May 1886 the scientists gathered at the Linnean Society were eager to hear Romanes' ideas. Romanes' strategy of sending announcements of his presentation to eminent scientist was successful, and the room was

---

[30] Letter from Romanes to Professor Raphael Meldola (from Meldola papers, Newham Museum Service, London), cited by Donald Forsdyke (http://post.queensu.ca/~forsdyke/romanes1.htm; Forsdyke, 2001, p. 221). Some years before, there had been a scientific discussion in *Nature* between Romanes and Meldola (Romanes, 1896, p. 93). Meldola was a supporter of Weismann, and had translated one of his main works: Weismann, August. *Studies in the Theory of Descent*. Translated by Raphael Meldola. 2 vols. London: Simpson Low, Marston, Searle and Rivington, 1882.

full: "There was a larger attendance than ever I saw there before" (Romanes to his sister Charlotte, May 1886, in: Romanes, 1896, p. 175).

There was another paper scheduled for that meeting. However, once the content of Romanes' contribution became known, the President of the Linnean Society (John Lubbock) withdrew the paper he was going to present in the same evening, so as to leave more time for the presentation and discussion of Romanes' long paper (Romanes, 1896, p. 175). Romanes' ideas were not well received[31], and produced a lot of criticism and debate: "I spoke for an hour and a half, and the discussion lasted another hour" (Romanes to his sister Charlotte, May 1886, in: Romanes, 1896, p. 175).

When one reads Romanes' paper, it is not difficult to perceive why it should bring about a strong wave of negative reaction. The very first paragraph of the communication read[32]:

> There can be no one to whom I yield in my veneration for the late Mr. Darwin, or in my appreciation of his work. But for this very reason I feel that in now venturing to adopt in some measure an attitude of criticism towards that work, a few words are needed to show that I have not done so hastily, or without due premeditation. (Romanes, 1886, p. 337)[33]

What should any one expect after this introduction? Romanes was clearly begging the public (or the readers) to forgive him, because he was going to criticize Darwin's work. He was unfortunate enough to use the very word "premeditation", so frequently applied to crimes[34]. All evidences suggested that the disciple was going to dishonor Darwin's memory. After listening to (or reading) this first paragraph,

---

[31] However, Romanes wrote to his sister: "The Linnean Society paper went off admirably" (Romanes to Charlotte, May 1886, in: Romanes, 1896, p. 175).

[32] The published version of Romanes' paper might be different from the communication he read at the Linnean Society, but it seems that he did not rewrite the original paper: after presentation and discussion, he just added a "Postscript" and sent it for publication.

[33] The second part of the present book contains the full text of Romanes' 1886 article, with indication of the original pages.

[34] "**pre-med-i-ta-tion** *n.* **1.** The act of speculating, arranging, or plotting in advance. **2.** *Law.* The contemplation and plotting of a crime in advance, showing intent to commit the crime" (Morris, 1975, p. 1034).

every Darwinian would feel an immediate strong prejudice against Romanes' proposal.

The second half of the next paragraph would not help to dismiss this first negative impression:

> It is now fifteen years since I became a close student of Darwinism, and during the greater part of that time I have had the privilege of discussing the whole philosophy of Evolution with Mr. Darwin himself. In the result I have found it impossible to entertain a doubt, either upon Evolution as a fact, or upon Natural Selection as a method. But during all these years it has seemed to me that there are certain weak points in the otherwise unassailable defences with which Mr. Darwin has fortified his citadel, or in the evidences with which he has surrounded his theory of natural selection. And the more I have thought upon these points, the greater has seemed the difficulty which they present; until at last I became satisfied that some cause, or causes, must have been at work in the production of species other than that of natural selection, and yet of an equally general kind. (Romanes, 1886, p. 337)

"Well, Mr. Romanes – someone could remark – so you have always doubted the theory of natural selection, even when you were a close associate of Mr. Darwin. And while he was always kind to you and helped your career, you were always collecting difficulties and are now *satisfied* that natural selection is not a sufficient explanation of the production of new species? And so, are you more ingenious than Darwin, since you have found now the solution of problems he was unable to answer?" The beginning of Romanes' paper must have brought a wave of thoughts like these.

On the whole, the rest of the paper is much milder than the beginning, but Romanes was not careful enough in his choice of words and sentences. There were several shocking remarks that could be interpreted as a complete break with Darwinism. For instance, Romanes stated that the was "drifting into this position of **scepticism** with regard to natural selection as in itself a full explanation of the origin of species" (Romanes, 1886, p. 337; my emphasis). Other sentences implied that Darwin's theory had been superseded or rejected, and that he was now criticizing the theory of natural selection:

> And since Mr. Darwin's death the tide of opinion continues to flow in this direction; so that at the present time it would be impossible to find any working naturalist who supposes that

> survival of the fittest is competent to explain all the phenomena of species-formation [...]. (Romanes, 1886, p. 337)

> Therefore, in now adopting an attitude of criticism towards certain portions of Mr. Darwin's work, I cannot feel that I am turning traitor to the cause of Darwinism. (Romanes, 1886, p. 338)

At other places, Romanes employed a different tone and endeavored to convince his audience that he was not opposing Darwin's theory, but offering a complementary explanation:

> On the contrary, I hope thus to remove certain difficulties in the way of Darwinian teaching; and I well know that Mr. Darwin himself would have been the first to welcome my attempt at suggesting another factor in the formation of species, which, although quite independent of natural selection, is in no way opposed to natural selection, and may therefore be regarded as a factor supplementary to natural selection. (Romanes, 1886, p. 338)

Whether consciously or not, Romanes used an aggressive language, stating that Darwin had *failed* to explain the mutual sterility of natural species:

> Mr. Darwin himself allows that this difference cannot be explained by natural selection; and indeed proves very clearly, as well as very candidly, that it must be due to causes hitherto undetected. As we shall presently find, he treats this difficulty at greater length and with more elaboration than any other; but, as we shall also find, **entirely fails** to overcome it. (Romanes, 1886, p. 338; my emphasis)

> Here, then, we have the core of the problem; and it is just here that **Mr. Darwin's explanations fail**. (Romanes, 1886, p. 342; my emphasis)

> In view of these considerations I conclude, that while Mr. Darwin has given the best of reasons to show why domesticated varieties have so rarely become sterile *inter se*, **he has entirely failed** to suggest any reason why this should so generally have been the case with natural species. (Romanes, 1886, p. 342)

More outrageous than Romanes' wording was the very content of his speech. After a long preamble, Romanes pointed out that the theory of natural selection could only account for useful changes – that is, natural selection was a theory explaining the origin of *adaptations*. However, sometimes species differ from one another by characters that are not conspicuously useful. Besides that, the main distinction of well-marked species is the infertility of the offspring of individuals belonging to different species. Darwin had admitted that this cross-infertility could not be explained by natural selection. The third difficulty was the possibility of divergent evolution that was very difficult to understand in the absence of geographical isolation. For all those reasons, Romanes boldly declared that Darwin's theory could not be regarded as a theory on the origin of species, and that Darwin's main book had been misnamed:

> In view of the foregoing considerations it appears to me obvious that **the theory of natural selection has been misnamed; it is not, strictly speaking, a theory of the origin of *species***: it is a theory of the origin – or rather of the cumulative development – of *adaptations*, whether these be morphological, physiological, or psychological, and whether they occur in species only, or likewise in genera, families, orders, and classes. (Romanes, 1886, p. 345; my emphasis)

> Again, it is comparatively seldom that we encounter any difficulty in perceiving the utilitarian significance of generic and family distinctions, while we still more rarely encounter any such difficulty in the case of ordinal and class distinctions. Why, then, should we often encounter this difficulty in the case of specific distinctions? Surely because some cause other than natural selection must have been at work in the differentiation of species, which has operated in a lesser degree in the differentiation of genera, and probably not at all in the differentiation of families, orders, and classes. Such a cause it is the object of the present paper to suggest; and if in the foregoing preamble it appears somewhat presumptuous to have insinuated that Mr. Darwin's great work on the 'Origin of Species' has been misnamed, I will conclude the preamble with a quotation from that work itself, which appears at once to justify the insinuation, and to concede all that I require. (Romanes, 1886, pp. 346-347)

The citation presented by Romanes[35] does not, of course, show that Darwin acknowledged that natural selection was not a theory on the origin of species. It shows that Darwin allowed that differences used by taxonomists to tell one species from another similar one are

---

[35] Darwin, 1872, p. 176.

usually of no adaptive value, that is, of little vital importance, and cannot therefore be explained by natural selection.

Let me quote some other passages where Romanes insisted in denying that Darwin's theory could explain the origin of species:

> Seeing that the theory of natural selection is confessedly unable to explain the primary specific distinction of sterility, as well as a large proportional number of the secondary specific distinctions; seeing also that, even as regards the remainder, it is difficult to see how natural selection alone could have evolved them in the presence of free intercrossing; seeing all this, **it becomes obvious that natural selection is not a theory of the origin of species**: it is a theory of the genesis of adaptive modifications, whether these happen to be distinctive of species only, or likewise of higher taxonomic divisions. (Romanes, 1886, pp. 397-398; my emphasis)

> Only, if species were always distinguishable in points of utilitarian significance, if natural selection were able fully to explain the fact of their mutual sterility, and if it were a part of the theory to show that in some way the mutual crossing of varieties is prevented; only under these circumstances could it be properly said that a theory of the genesis of adaptive modifications is likewise a theory of the origin of species. But, as matters stand, supplementary theories are required. (Romanes, 1886, p. 398)

Leaving the rhetorical features aside, Romanes did present nice arguments for his idea that natural selection *alone* was unable to explain several features concerning the origin of species. Darwin himself had allowed that besides natural selection there were some supplementary natural causes of organic evolution, such as use and disuse, sexual selection, correlated variability, prolonged exposure to similar conditions of life, prevention of intercrossing by geographical barriers (or by migration). However, Romanes claimed that none of those auxiliary causes was able to explain the above-described problems. That was his excuse for proposing the theory of physiological selection.

According to Romanes, closely allied species can only originate from a common ancestral species if they become isolated from one another, in such a way as to prevent intercrossing. Geographical barriers can sometimes produce this effect. However, geographical barriers do not always separate closely allied species, and Romanes suggested that the initial step in the origin of new species could be a variation that produced a partial or total cross-infertility which prevented intercrossing with the parent form.

The aim of Romanes' paper was not to deny that natural selection was the main cause of evolution, but to propose a new, independent factor, that was in no way opposed to natural selection but that could explain facts that presented a difficulty to Darwin's theory.

If one states Romanes' ideas in those terms, his proposal seems acceptable. However, returning to his own way of expounding his own achievement, we find out that he boasted having solved the greatest of all mysteries, the origin of species:

> Whatever, therefore, may be thought as to the truth of this theory, or as to the extent of its applicability, it is certainly something very much more than a bare re-statement of fact. If the evidence which I have presented on these points is accepted. (as it must be by the criticism with which I am dealing), the explanatory value of the theory may be estimated by the consideration that what Mr. Darwin has called the "mystery of mysteries" * ceases to be mysterious in any other sense or degree than the general fact that offspring do not always and in every respect resemble their parents. (Romanes, 1886, p. 411)

Romanes did not have at the time sufficient evidence for his theory. He claimed that some observations and experiments (that he described in his paper) could lead to a definite decision concerning his theory: "It only remains to be said that the theory of physiological selection has this immense advantage over every other theory that has ever been propounded on the origin of species: it admits of being either demonstrated or destroyed by verification" (Romanes, 1886, p. 403).

He thought it would take many years to collect the relevant facts and to perform the experiments to check the theory. Toward the end of his paper, he asked for the help of other naturalists: "In view of this consideration, I have deemed it best to publish my theory before undertaking the labour of verification; for, by so doing, I hope to induce other naturalists to cooperate with me in carrying on the research in different parts of the world" (Romanes, 1886, p. 403).

---

* Romanes' footnote: "Viz. – the problem of the origin of species, which, as shown in the preceding paper, his theory of natural selection serves only in small part to explain".

Reaction against Romanes

What reaction did Romanes expect from his speech at the Linnean Society? We have no documented evidence that he anticipated an easy and general acceptance. However, the careless language he used in the paper strongly suggests that he counted on a sympathetic reception, and Romanes' correspondence shows that he did not anticipate such a negative reaction as was witnessed after his talk.

Let us try to reconstruct Romanes' expectations. If he could convince his fellow scientists that Darwin's theory was unable to explain the origin of species, and that he, Romanes, had a nice theory to account for that origin and to solve several difficulties of Darwin's theory, he would be regarded as the most competent evolutionist of his time.

However, Romanes' tactics was not successful. Besides being criticized in the discussion at the Linnean Society, he soon received letters blaming his attitude. The general opinion was against him.

Wallace soon published a criticism of Romanes' paper in the *Fortnightly Review* (Wallace, 1886) with the title "Romanes *versus* Darwin". The theory of physiological selections was also criticized at the British Association meeting, in August 1886:

> Physiological selection seems to have brought a regular nest of hornets about my head. If I had known there was to have been so much talk about it at the British Association I should have gone up to defend the new-born. (Romanes to Meldola, 16/Sept./86, in: Romanes, 1896, p. 176)

In the following years, Romanes had to justify and explain himself many times, because his proposal was regarded by several scientists (not unreasonably) as an attack against Darwin's theory. In a letter to his opponent Thielson Dyer[36], for instance, Romanes tried to elucidate his own opinion:

> Read in the light of subsequent experience, I have no doubt that I ought to have expressed myself with more care while writing my

---

[36] William Thiselton-Dyer (1843-1928) was the Director (1885-1905) of the Royal Botanic Gardens, Kew.

> paper. But, to tell the honest truth, it never once occurred to me that I of all men could be suspected of trying to undermine the theories of Darwin. I was entirely filled with the one idea of presenting what seemed to me 'a supplementary hypothesis', which, while 'in no way opposed to natural selection', would 'release the latter from the only difficulties' which to my mind it had ever presented. Therefore I took it for granted that everybody would go with me in recognising natural selection as the 'boss' round which every 'other theory' must revolve, without my having to say so on every page. So, of course, by 'other theory' I did not mean that physiological selection was in my opinion the *only* theory of the origin of species. Everywhere throughout the paper, from the title-page to the conclusion, I represent it as an 'additional suggestion', a 'supplementary hypothesis', &c., &c. Sexual selection is in my view. (as it is also in Darwin's, Wallace's, and doubtless that of all evolutionists) one of the 'other theories that have been propounded on the origin of species'. So is Lamarck's theory, which was considered by Darwin as *more or less* 'supplementary' to natural selection; and this is all that I meant [...] by speaking of physiological selection as another theory of the origin of species. (Romanes to Dyer, 7/Jan./89, in: Romanes, 1896, pp. 218-219)

The reaction against Romanes' work was much stronger in England than in other countries – probably because abroad the emotional factors were much milder.

> It is most astonishing to me with what a storm of opposition this idea has been met in England, and how persistent is the misunderstanding. In Germany and America it is being much more fairly treated, but meanwhile I intend to keep it as quiet as possible, till I shall be in a position to publish a large body of experimental observations. As far as time has hitherto allowed, the results are strongly corroborative of the theory. (Romanes to Le Conte, 21/Jan./89, in: Romanes, 1896, p. 242)

Several years later (a few months before his death), Romanes still complained that he was not understood in England:

> I have, indeed, often wondered how you and ——— and ——— can have so persistently misunderstood my ideas, seeing that neither on the Continent nor in America has there been any difficulty in making myself intelligible. (Romanes to Dyer, 26/Sept./93, in: Romanes, 1896, p. 344)

What was Francis Darwin's reaction? We do not know. It is likely that Romanes had talked to him in advance of the Linnean Society talk, and that he was sympathetic to Romanes' work. However, Romanes' correspondence presents evidence that he was anxious to obtain his support for his views (Romanes to Francis Darwin, 5/Nov./86 and 7/Jan./87 in: Romanes, 1896, pp. 178-184).

Although Romanes stressed (after the presentation of his paper) that physiological selection was compatible with natural selection, he admitted that the new theory deviated from Darwin's own work: "Of course I might have said more about the swamping effects of free intercrossing (which appears to me the only point in which I deviate at all from the 'Origin of species') [...]" (Romanes to Francis Darwin, 7/Jan./87, in: Romanes, 1896, p. 180). Indeed, Romanes' proposal was an *alternative* to Darwin's own explanation of the way new species could arise without geographical isolation (Darwin, 1872, chapter 4). Romanes acknowledged that in this point his theory was not a mere *addition* to the theory of natural selection:

> As for my having attributed too much to the swamping effects of intercrossing. (Panmixia), this, I am convinced, is the one and only particular wherein I have at all departed from the judgments of Darwin; though, curiously enough, it is the particular on which my critics have laid least stress when accusing me of Darwinian heresy. (Romanes to Dyer, 7/Jan./89, in: Romanes, 1896, pp. 221-222)

Relevant tests of physiological selection

According to the theory of physiological selection, closely related species in immediate contact (with no geographical barrier) should be at least partially sterile as regards each other, while closely related species isolated by geographical barriers (nearby islands or mountains) needed not be mutually sterile. Romanes thought that confirmation of those predictions would help to win new adepts for his theory. He couldn't find sufficient information on this subject, however. Hence, he tried to obtain the help of other scientists to check his theory of physiological selection:

> My object in now writing – over and above that of thanking you for your paper – is to ask whether you yourself, or any other American naturalist whom you may know, would not feel it well worth while to try some experiments on the hybridisation of the peculiar species. [...] And I should expect him to find marked evidence of mutual sterility between closely allied unique species growing on the same island, with possibly unimpaired fertility between allied species growing on different islands. If this anticipation should be realised by experiment, the fact would go far to prove my theory. (Romanes to Le Conte, 11/Oct./87, in: Romanes, 1896, p. 238)

He also wrote to his critic, Thiselton Dyer, looking for relevant references:

> Would you mind sending me on a postcard the name of the genus of plants the constituent species of which you alluded to in the train as being mutually fertile, and also separated from one another topographically? I want to get as many of such cases as I possibly can, so, if any others occur to you, please mention them likewise.
> By reading pages 401 and 404 of my paper, you will see why such cases are of quite as much importance to me as the converse, viz. Where closely allied species inhabiting *continuous* areas are more or less mutually sterile. (Romanes to Dyer, 20/Dec./88, in: Romanes, 1896, p. 209)

A relevant test of physiological selection would be an attempt to produce hybrids by crossing closely related species of plants growing on the top of different mountains. According to Romanes, they would prove to be mutually fertile, in general. That seemed to him a very important test, and for that reason he helped to establish an experimental garden in the Alps to check his predictions:

> *Re* physiological selection. I have sent Correvon, of Geneva, £50 to help in funding a garden in the Alps. Which will have the proud distinction of being the highest in the world. He is a splendid man for his knowledge of Alpine Flora, and besides, is strongly bitten with a desire to test physiological selection. Of course I shall do the hybridising experiments myself, but he will collect the material from the different mountains – *i.e.* nearly allied species, topographically separated, and therefore, I hope, mutually fertile. The converse experiments of nearly allied species on common areas may be tried in England. (Romanes to Francis Darwin, 20/Jan./89, in: Romanes, 1896, p. 216)

> There are none so blind as those who will not see. Where can your powers of 'observation' have been when you can still remark that I ignore the facts of hybridisation? I can only repeat that from the first I have regarded them as evidence of the utmost importance as establishing a highly general correlation between *separate* origin of allied species and *absence* of cross-sterility. In fact, for the last five years I have had experiments going on in my Alpine garden, which I helped in founding for the very purpose of inquiring into this matter. And Focke, with whom I have been in correspondence from the first, and who *does* understand the theory, writes that in his opinion it will 'solve the whole mystery' of natural hybridisation in relation to artificial. (Romanes to Dyer, 15/Sept./93, in: Romanes, 1896, pp. 340-341)

In the years following the presentation of his paper (1886) Romanes obtained many evidences favorable to his theory, as he put it to Dyer, one year before his death:

> In fact, as stated over and over again in my original paper, *this* correlation between geographical isolation and cross-fertility is *one* of my lines of verification, the *other* line being the correlation between identical stations and cross-sterility.
>
> Now, as above state, I have found both these correlations to obtain in a surprisingly general manner.
>
> I wish that, instead of perpetually misunderstanding the theory, you English botanists would help me by pointing out *exceptions* to

these two rules, so that I might specially investigate them. It seems to me that the group you name goes to corroborate the first of them, while all Jordan's work, for instance, uniformly bears out the second. And whatever may be thought about him in other respects, I am not aware that anyone has ever refuted his observations and experiments so far as I am concerned with them. (Romanes to Dyer, 15/June/93, in: Romanes, 1896, p. 332)

The search for positive evidences of the theory of physiological selection was the most important scientific work Romanes undertook in the late part of his life. He expected that it would be possible to provide a firm empirical foundation for this theory, and that the theory would be finally accepted. Romanes' wife remarked: "This theory was very close to his heart, and perhaps no part of his work was left unfinished with more keen regret" (Romanes, 1896, p. 185). When Romanes fell severely ill and was confronted with his eminent death, he wrote to Dyer and to Huxley:

Since my last letter to you I have been at death's door. On July 11, I was struck down by paralysis of the left side, and am now a wreck. Not the least of my sorrow is that I fear I shall have to leave the verification of phys. sel. to other hands in larger measure than I had hoped. I have little doubt that it will eventually prevail; but more time will probably be needed before it does. (Romanes to Dyer, 15/Sept./93, in: Romanes, 1896, pp. 340-341)

[...] although I have now recovered to the extent of being able to crawl about a little, I am but a wreck of my former self. Moreover the doctors prohibit work of every kind, so that my misery is absolute, all my experiments have come to an untimely end, and it is improbable that any of my half-written books can ever be published.

I am most of all disappointed about my theory of 'Physiological Selection', for which I have accumulated a large mass of evidence during the last seven years, and which I had hoped would satisfy most people as an explanation of the contrast between natural species and artificial varieties in respect of cross-sterility. (Romanes to Huxley, 26/Sept./93, in: Romanes, 1896, p. 343)

So, Romanes regarded this theory – and its foundation – as the summit of his scientific work. Had he been able to provide a firm basis for physiological selection, and to convince the scientific community to accept it, he would regard his scientific work as complete. However, after proposing the theory of physiological selection, Romanes devoted himself to other enterprises. It is necessary to analyze those other lines of work in order to understand fully Romanes' professional strategy.

Darwin, and after Darwin

Presenting popular courses and writing popular accounts of Darwin's theory should be a relevant part of the strategy of anyone attempting to become the spokesman of Darwinism. It seems that Romanes was a successful lecturer, but since he was not attached to any university[37] he had scanty opportunity of presenting himself in public: only a few invited talks, and presentations at meetings of scientific societies[38]. His more technical works were read and discussed by just a few specialists. Outside a very small circle, he was not well known.

This situation began to change after Darwin's death, however. In 1886 Romanes was invited to deliver a series of lectures on "The philosophy of natural history" at the University of Edinburgh. Romanes held this lectureship for five years. He first delivered a series of talks on the history of biology[39]. Afterwards, he lectured on the theories of Lamarck, Darwin, and post-Darwinian theories. This series of lectures was shortly afterward developed in a three-year course he delivered at the Royal Institution[40] (Romanes, 1896, p. 186). Each yearly course at the Royal Institution comprised between 30 and 40 lectures (Romanes, 1892-1897, p. v).

> The Institution lectures give much more satisfaction than I anticipated, as I thought the historical character of this year's course would appeal but to a small number of people. But the audience keeps up to between one hundred and two hundred very steadily. (usually one hundred and fifty), and is in part made up of outsiders.

---

[37] Only towards the end of his life, in 1890, he accepted an invitation to join the Oxford University.

[38] For instance, he lectured in the Royal Institution in January 1883 (Romanes, 1896, p. 155).

[39] Romanes never tried to publish this part of his lectures: "Of these the first – of that which deals with the purely historical side of biological science – may be allowed to stand over for an indefinite time" (Romanes, 1896-1897, vol. 1, p. vi).

[40] The lectures given in the Royal Institution from 1888 to 1890 had the title "Before and after Darwin" (Romanes, 1896-1897, vol. 1, p. v).

(Romanes to his sister Charlotte, 18/May/88, in: Romanes, 1896, p. 195)

Lecturing gave him much gratification. Besides that, the lectures provided the stimulus for reviewing most evolutionary works published before and after Darwin. He soon decided to write a series of books where he was to present his own view on the theory of descent in a general and systematic way. And so he designed his plan to publish what was to become his last work: *Darwin, and after Darwin: an exposition of the Darwinian theory and a discussion of post-Darwinian questions.*

Why did Romanes feel that it was necessary to discuss the theories that had arisen after Darwin's death? According to Romanes, there were "several divergent schools of thought which have arisen since Darwin's death", regarding different opinions on this point: "whether natural selection has been the sole, or but the main, cause of organic evolution" (Romanes, 1892-1897, vol. 2, p. 1). However, different views existed already before Darwin's death. Wallace only accepted natural selection; Spencer (and Häckel) strongly emphasized use-inheritance. What was really new after Darwin's death was that evolutionists declared war to one another, attempting to take hold of the Master's mantle[41]. Darwinians were fighting among themselves, and not against anti-evolutionists or against those who clearly criticized Darwin and suggested that natural selection was of no significance.

In the second volume of *Darwin, and after Darwin*, Romanes did not discuss anti-evolutionists. He did not address, either, other evolutionary views of the time, such as discontinuous "jumps" and the hypothesis of an internal drive toward perfection. He refers to neo-Lamarckians, but they do not seem to disturb him, and he does not criticize their views. Indeed, his whole concern is with other Darwinians.

Neo-Darwinism,[42] the school associated to Weismann's name, was the strongest Darwinian view after Darwin's death. It is understandable that Romanes attempted to criticize this view, not neo-Lamarckians or anti-evolutionist. Indeed, Romanes was struggling for scientific recognition, and struggle for recognition, as

---

[41] Romanes sometimes referred to Darwin as "the Master".

[42] The phrase "Neo-Darwinism" was coined by Romanes in 1889.

struggle for life, is more severe between individuals and varieties of the same species[43].

The first volume of *Darwin, and after Darwin* appeared in the spring of 1892. According to Romanes, it intended to present an account of Darwinism accessible to general readers. Books on evolution were usually poor in illustrations – Darwin's *Origin of species* had only a few diagrams. Häckel's books had introduced several nice drawings, but Romanes was the first English-language author to publish an illustrated account of the theory of evolution (there were 125 figures in the first volume of *Darwin, and after Darwin*)[44].

> Nevertheless, I desire it to be understood that the first part of this treatise is intended to retain its original character, as a merely educational exposition of Darwinian teaching – an exposition, therefore, which, in its present form, may be regarded as a compendium, or hand-book, adapted to the requirements of a general reader, or biological student, as distinguished from those of a professed naturalist. (Romanes, 1892-1897, vol. 1, p. 10)

However, the book was not a mere popularization of Darwin's thought: it was to present the *correct* view of Darwinism.

> As the present volume is thus intended to be merely a systematic exposition of what may be termed the Darwinism of Darwin, and as on this account it is likely to prove of more service to general readers than to professed naturalists, I have been everywhere careful to avoid assuming even the most elementary knowledge of natural science on the part of those to whom the exposition is addressed. (Romanes, 1892-1897, vol. 1, p. vi)

It is very easy to ascertain what Romanes had in view when he wrote that he was going to present "the Darwinism of Darwin". In

---

[43] "But the struggle will almost invariably be most severe between individuals of the same species, for they frequent the same districts, require the same food, and are exposed to the same dangers"; "As the species of the same genus usually have, though by no means invariably, much similarity in habits and constitution, and always in structure, the struggle will generally be more severe between them, if they come into competition with each other, than between the species of distinct genera" (Darwin, 1872, pp. 58, 59).

[44] In 1892, Romanes published a popular, illustrated book on Darwin's theory of evolution: *Darwinism illustrated; wood-engravings explanatory of the theory of evolution*. The biography written by Romanes' wife nowhere mentions this book.

1889 Wallace had published a book called *Darwinism: an exposition of the theory of natural selection, with some of its applications* (1889), which Romanes immediately criticized (Romanes, 1889).

> As it was, Wallace's stubborn insistence upon equating his evolutionary theory with "Darwinism," was more obfuscating than elucidating. By doing so he consigned himself to the obscurity that the Darwinian banner would surely hold for him. It was exacerbated when George John Romanes, who sought to assume the mantle of leadership following Darwin's death, accused Wallace, quite misleadingly, of "ultra-Darwinism" for his strict selectionist views. (Flannery, 2011, p. 84)

Romanes also intended to use *Darwin, and after Darwin* to function as an introduction for his own theory, and he justified his approach as a denial of dogmatism:

> For while not a few naturalists have since erred on the side of insufficiently distinguishing between fully verified principles of evolution and merely speculative deductions therefrom, a still larger number have formed for themselves a Darwinian creed, and regard any further theorizing on the subject of evolution as *ipso facto* unorthodox.
>
> [...] No one in this generation is able to imitate Darwin, either as an observer or a generalizer. But this does not hinder that we should all so far endeavour to follow his *method*, as always to draw a clear distinction, not merely between observation and deduction, but also between degrees of verification. At all events, my own aim will everywhere be to avoid dogmatism on the one hand, and undue timidity as regards general reasoning on the other. (Romanes, 1892-1897, vol. 1, p. 8)

So, instead of presenting Darwin's Darwinism, Romanes' final aim was to present *his own Darwinism*. Of course, he believed that his own views would ultimately gain general acceptance:

> But although a great deal must thus be necessarily lost on the one side, I am disposed to think that more will be gained on the other, by presenting, in a terser form than would otherwise be possible, the whole theory of organic evolution **as I believe that it will eventually stand**. (Romanes, 1892-1897, vol. 1, p. 9; my emphasis)

Romanes wanted to reach not only the general public, but also younger naturalists, attempting to persuade them to abandon what he regarded as the wrong Darwinian creed:

> Now the only difference between such naturalists [those of Darwin's time] and their successors of the present day is, that the latter have grown up in a Darwinian environment, and so, as already remarked, have more or less thoughtlessly adopted some form of Darwinism creed. But this scientific creed is not a whit less dogmatic and intolerant than was the more theological one which it has supplanted; and while it usually incorporates the main elements of Darwin's teaching, it still more usually comprises gross perversions of their consequences. (Romanes, 1892-1897, vol. 1, pp. 11-12)

In *Darwin, and after Darwin* Romanes also attempted to undermine the status of some well-known authors. One of his targets was Herbert Spencer.

Herbert Spencer had been arguing for evolutionary ideas since 1851, when he published an essay calling the attention to and defending Lamarck's work (Bowler, 1990, p. 169). After the publication of the *Origin of species* he had also accepted natural selection, but he still believed that use-disuse and inheritance of acquired characters was the main cause of evolutionary change (Bowler, 1989, pp. 238-241). When Weismann began to argue for a kind of Darwinism without use-inheritance, Spencer wrote against this approach (Bowler, 1990, p. 171).

Spencer was a highly influential author. He was one of the few British candidates to the leadership of evolutionary thought after Darwin's decease. In order to undermine his status, Romanes put Herbert Spencer in the same group as Erasmus Darwin and Lamarck – as a supporter of the pre-Darwinian theory of use-inheritance (Romanes, 1892-1897, vol. 1, p. 253). Romanes then clearly stated that the Lamarckian theory "even if it be supposed to present any truth at all, is clearly insufficient as a full or complete theory of organic evolution" (Romanes, 1892-1897, vol. 1, p. 256). After that, Romanes mentioned the principle of natural selection, and again referred to Herbert Spencer: "Still more remarkable is the fact that Mr. Herbert Spencer – notwithstanding his great powers of abstract thought and his great devotion of those powers to the theory of evolution, when as yet this theory was scorned by science – still more remarkable, I say, is the fact that Mr. Herbert Spencer should have missed what now appears so obvious an idea" (Romanes, 1892-1897, vol. 1, p. 257).

Did Romanes reject the "Lamarckian factors"? No, he clearly accepted them to the very time of his death, and he many times recalled that Darwin also accepted them. Why, then, was he emphasizing that Spencer was a supporter of use-inheritance as a negative trait of his work? This attitude can only be interpreted as a strategic rhetorical trick to lessen the respectability of a competitor, since Romanes himself did not stick in a rigid way to natural selection. Although he used the weight of natural selection against Spencer, he also stressed that this theory should not be regarded as a solution of all evolutionary problems:

> Of all errors connected with the theory of natural selection, perhaps the one most frequently met with – especially among supporters of the theory – is that of employing the theory to explain all cases of phyletic modification. (or inherited change of type) indiscriminately, without waiting to consider whether in particular cases its application is so much as logically possible. The term "natural selection" thus becomes a magic work, or Sesame, at the utterance of which every closed door is supposed to be immediately opened. Be it observed, I am not here alluding to that merely blind faith in natural selection, which of late years has begun dogmatically to force this principle as the sole cause of organic evolution in every case it is *logically possible* that the principle can come into play. Such a blind faith, indeed, I hold to be highly inimical, not only to the progress of biological science, but even to the true interests of the natural selection theory itself. As to this I shall have a good deal to say in the next volume. Here, however, the point is, that the theory in question is often invoked in cases where it is not even logically possible that it can apply, and therefore in cases where its application betokens, not merely an error of judgment or extravagance of dogmatism, but a fallacy of reasoning in the nature of a logical contradiction. Almost any number of examples might be given; but one will suffice to illustrate what is meant. And I choose it from the writings of one of the authors of the selection theory itself, in order to show how easy it is to be cheated by this mere juggling with a phrase – for of course I do not doubt that a moment's thought would have shown the writer the untenability of his statement. (Romanes, 1892-1897, vol. 1, p. 271)

Why did Romanes stress that one should not adhere in a dogmatic way to natural selection? He had two main motives for that emphasis.

First, because his own proposal of physiological selection was a complement to Darwin's theory, and could only be accepted if one interpreted natural selection as the main, but not the exclusive, cause of organic change. Secondly, Romanes used this interpretation of Darwin's theory to undermine Wallace's views, which amounted to say that the only factor of organic evolution was natural selection. Accordingly, immediately after the above quoted passage, Romanes presented a detailed criticism of Wallace.

Romanes pointed out many misconceptions of Darwin's theory presented by the *critics* of natural selection (see, for instance, Romanes, 1892-1897, vol. 1, chapter 9). However, he dealt at greater length with faulty interpretations by those who *defended* Darwinism. Why did he do that? It is likely that his main intent was to establish himself as the only Darwinian who was faithful to Darwin, and therefore it was necessary to attack other Darwinians, but it would be less useful to attack anti-Darwinians.

Romanes pointed out several statements that he regarded as *misinterpretations* of the theory of natural selection (Romanes, 1892-1897, vol. 1, pp. 273-277). Three of them were central features of Wallace's interpretation:
1. That it follows from the theory that all adaptive changes must be due to natural selection.
2. That all hereditary characters are necessarily due to natural selection.
3. Therefore [as consequence of the former statements] natural selection is the only possible cause of modification, whether adaptive or non-adaptive.

Romanes discussed the common objections to Darwin's theory, and attempted to show that they were usually due to a misunderstanding of the theory. However, there are three objections with a special status in his view:

> The three objections to which I allude are,. (1) that a large proportional number of specific, as well as of higher taxonomic characters, are seemingly useless characters, and therefore do not send themselves to explanation by the Darwinian theory;. (2) that the most general of all specific characters – viz. Cross-infertility between allied species – cannot possibly be due to natural selection, as is demonstrated by Darwin himself;. (3) that the swamping effects of free intercrossing must always render impossible by

natural selection alone any evolution of species in divergent. (as distinguished from serial) lines of change. (Romanes, 1892-1897, vol. 1, p. 374)

> These three objections have been urged from time to time by not a few of the most eminent botanists and zoologists of our century; and from one point of view I cannot myself have the smallest doubt that the objections thus advanced are not only valid in themselves, but also by far the most formidable objections which the theory of natural selection has encountered. From another point of view, however, I am equally convinced that they all admit of absolute annihilation. (Romanes, 1892-1897, vol. 1, p. 374)

Romanes then goes on to explain that, if natural selection is regarded as the *sole* cause of organic change, then the three difficulties are insurmountable; but that they can be answered if one regards natural selection as the main but not the only factor of organic evolution (Romanes, 1892-1897, vol. 1, p. 375). He promised to discuss those objections in the following volume of his work[45]. Those are exactly the three points he presented in his article on physiological selection, to support his hypothesis.

At this point, Romanes emphasized that those difficulties would be insuperable for Wallace, but not for Darwin:

> [...] no one of these facts is entitled to rank as an objection against the theory of natural selection, unless we understand this theory to claim an exclusive prerogative in the field of organic evolution. This, as we have previously seen, is what Mr. Wallace does claim for it; while on the other hand, Mr. Darwin expressly – and even vehemently – repudiates the claim[46]: from which it follows that all the three main objections against the theory of natural selection are objections which vitally affect the theory only as it has been stated and upheld by Wallace. (Romanes, 1892-1897, vol. 1, pp. 375-376)

> All these the most formidable objections against the theory of natural selection arise simply and solely from what I conceive to be

---

[45] Of course, the solution of those difficulties was, according to Romanes, physiological selection. He first intended to include that theory in the second volume of *Darwin, and after Darwin*. Afterwards, he decided to devote a third volume to physiological selection.

[46] A few pages ahead, Romanes quoted Darwin's famous sentence: "I am convinced that natural selection has been the main, but not the exclusive, means of modification" (Romanes, 1892-1897, vol. 1, p. 378).

the erroneous manner in which the theory has been presented by Darwin's distinguished colleague. (Romanes, 1892-1897, vol. 1, p. 376)

As shown above, when Romanes published his 1886 paper on physiological selection, he had presented those objections as *difficulties of Darwin's theory*, and this gave rise to his being described as standing against Darwin. Now he claimed that this interpretation was a misunderstanding (Romanes, 1892-1897, vol. 1, p. 376), and now he was sufficiently clever to divert all criticism from Darwin and concentrate his weapons against Wallace.

After discussing natural selection, Romanes turned to sexual selection (Romanes, 1892-1897, vol. 1, chapter 10). He described the main lines of the theory, and then he called the attention of the readers to the circumstance that sexual selection was an *additional theory*, attempting to explain a class of facts that Darwin could not ascribe to natural selection, and therefore "wholly and completely distinct from the theory of natural selection" (Romanes, 1892-1897, vol. 1, p. 384). And then Romanes criticized Wallace again:

> We may next proceed to consider the objections which have been brought against the theory of sexual selection. And this is virtually the same thing as saying that we may now consider Mr. Wallace's views upon the subject. (Romanes, 1892-1897, vol. 1, p. 391)

Romanes discussed the objections brought by Wallace against sexual selection in his work *Tropical nature and other essays* (1878), and remarked:

> Unfortunately the work in which they [Wallace's objections] are mainly presented was published several years after the second edition of the *Descent of man*, so that Mr. Darwin never had a suitable opportunity of replying. But, if he had had such an opportunity, as far as I can judge it seems that his reply would have been more or less as follows. (Romanes, 1892-1897, vol. 1, p. 393)

> I have now briefly answered all Mr. Wallace's objections to this supplementary theory, and, as previously remarked, I feel pretty confident that, at all events in the main, the answer is such as Mr. Darwin would himself have supplied, had there been a third edition of his work upon the subject. [...] for his very last words to science – read only a few hours before his death at a meeting of the Zoological Society – were:

> "It may perhaps be here permitted to say that, after having carefully weighed, to the best of my ability, the various arguments which have been advanced against the principle of sexual selection, I remain firmly convinced of its truth.". (Romanes, 1892-1897, vol. 1, p. 400)

This is a strategy Romanes used many times: he counterfactually claimed that *had Darwin commented upon a given subject, he would have said such and such*. That is, Romanes used a fictitious Darwin to support his own claims. Of course, I am not stating that Romanes' interpretation of Darwin's thought was *wrong*. I am just stressing that this was a useful tactic Romanes made use of.

The first volume of *Darwin, and after Darwin* was of strategic value for Romanes, as it provided:
1. A way of being widely known as a defender of Darwinism;
2. A way to have access to biological students, influencing their views on evolution;
3. A way to present his interpretation of Darwinism, opening the way to the acceptance of his own theory of physiological selection;
4. A way to criticize other evolutionists, in an attempt to become the topmost Darwinist.

An examination of Weismannism

August Weismann was not one of the topmost evolutionists in the period preceding Darwin's death. However, in 1883 he rejected use-inheritance (Mayr preferred the phrase "soft inheritance") and claimed that natural selection was the sole cause of evolutionary change (Mayr, 1982, p. 538).

> The evolutionists presented a rather solid front as long as they still had to convince the world of the fact of evolution. This was largely true until about 1882, the year of Darwin's death. In the next twenty years, however, more and more events took place which sowed seeds of dissension among them. The first of these was Weismann's uncompromising rejection of any inheritance of acquired characters. The reaction which this provoked was a hardening of the claims of the neo-Lamarckians. (Mayr, 1982, p. 540)

That was a major move, and he soon obtained several British supporters. Before Darwin's death, only Wallace and, to a lesser extent, Bates and Hooker, argued that natural selections was sufficient to explain all the features of organic evolution. After Weismann's change of opinion, Edward Poulton, Raphael Meldola, Ray Lankester and other young scientists also accepted the all-sufficiency of natural selection (Mayr, 1982, p. 535).

It seems that Romanes regarded the rise of Weismannism as a serious threat to the Darwinian tradition and to his own ambitions. He started his campaign against Weismann in his Edinburgh lectures; and in 1890 his lectures at the Royal Institution were also on Weismann's theory.

Edward B. Poulton was one of the main supporters of Weismann's ideas in England. He was one of the translators of the *Essays upon heredity and kindred biological problems* (Weismann, 1889) and defended Weismann's ideas in press and in public presentations. A clash between Romanes and Poulton occurred in 1889:

> In 1889 Mr. Romanes attended the British Association which met that year at Newcastle. Here, he and Professor Poulton had a long discussion on the 'Inheritance of Acquired Characters'; he

spoke so much, and was so much *en évidence*, at this Association that the Newcastle papers described him as a most belligerent person. (Romanes, 1896, p. 202)

Of course, Romanes attempted to convince some key persons to back his opinion. In a letter to Francis Darwin, Romanes criticized Wallace's opposition to sexual selection and remarked:

> My own belief is, that what Lankester calls the 'pure Darwinians' are doing the same thing in another direction. By endeavouring, with Wallace and Weismann, to make natural selection all in all as the sole cause of adaptive structure, and expressly discarding the Darwinian recognition of use and disuse, I think they are doing harm to natural selection theory itself. Moreover, because I do not see any sufficient reason as yet to budge from the real Darwinian standpoint. (Weismann has added nothing to the facts which were known to Charles Darwin), the post-Darwinians accuse me of moving away from Darwinian principles. But it is they who are moving, and, because they see a change in our relative positions, affirm that it is I. (Romanes to Francis Darwin, 20/Jan./89, in: Romanes, 1896, p. 215)

In his correspondence Romanes also attempted to convince other scientists to abandon Weismann's theory, by arguing that Darwin would not agree with those ideas, if he were still alive:

> If there be no difference between Panmixia and Cessation of Selection, from what I have briefly sketched about it, it follows that, had Darwin lived till now, he would almost certainly have been opposed to Weismann. This is not a thing I should like to say in public, but one that I should like to feel practically assured about in my own mind. (Romanes to Poulton, 11/Nov./89, in: Romanes, 1896, p. 230)

The discussion of Weismann's ideas was to be part of the second volume of *Darwin, and after Darwin*. However, Romanes found two problems. One of them was that Weismann kept changing and improving his theory in successive works, and therefore it was difficult to publish an up-to-date criticism. In 1891 Weismann published his essay on *Amphimixis*, and soon afterwards *The germ-plasm* (1893)[47], where he presented new views on heredity and evolution.

---

[47] The German edition of the book was published in 1892.

In 1892 a large part of the second volume of *Darwin and after Darwin* was almost ready to be printed, when Romanes had serious health problems. At that time he decided to publish a separate book on Weismann's work, including all the chapters he had already prepared for the second volume of *Darwin and after Darwin*, but adding new chapters discussing some of Weismann's later ideas. So was born the book *An examination of Weismannism* (1892).

Weismann's theory of heredity had as it main foundation the denial of the inheritance of acquired characters. However, Romanes chose not to discuss this point in this book, reserving it for the second volume of *Darwin, and after Darwin*:

> As regards Weismannism, you will see that I have not dealt with the question of acquired characters in my 'Examination'. For, as this question has been vividly before me during half my life, I cannot allow that it belongs to 'Weismannism'. (Romanes to Huxley, 26/Sept./93, in: Romanes, 1896, p. 343)

Romanes regarded any negative evidence as inconclusive, because strict logic teaches us that the non-observation of a phenomenon does not prove that it does not exist. Besides that, most of Weismann's arguments against the inheritance of acquired characters were theoretical, and on that account Romanes remarked:

> It must be understood, however, that under the term 'Weismannism" I do not include any reference to the important question with which the name of Weismann has been mainly associated – i.e., the inheritance or non-inheritance of acquired characters. This is a question of fact, which stands to be answered by the inductive methods of observation and experiment[48]: not by the deductive methods of general reasoning. (Romanes, 1896, p. vii)

Romanes' *Examination of Weismannism* is a masterpiece of scientific controversy. The author explored every weak feature of Weismann's work – difficulties in applying the concept of the germplasm to plants, the successive changes of Weismann's ideas,

---

[48] Romanes referred to his old experiments on pangenesis: "As far back as 1874 I had long conversations with Darwin himself upon the matter [transmission of acquired characters], and under his guidance performed what I suppose are the only systematic experiments which have ever been undertaken with regard to it. These occupied more than five years of almost exclusive devotion; but, as they all proved failures, they were never published" (Romanes, 1896, p. viii).

contradictions, etc. Romanes cleverly summoned Darwin's spirit to take part of the battle. He pictured Weismann's theory of the germplasm and Darwin's pangenesis as "the logical extremes of explanatory thought" (Romanes, 1896, p. 1), calling the attention of his readers to the incompatibility of Weismann's work with some of Darwin's dearest assumptions.

Weismann's theory of the germplasm directly conflicted with Darwin's hypothesis of pangenesis. Romanes presented in his book a clear account of pangenesis, using it against Weismann. However, one could doubt whether Romanes still believed that pangenesis was a correct hypothesis, after his unsuccessful attempts to prove it.

There is some evidence that even after Darwin's death, Romanes continued to believe that pangenesis was a sound hypothesis. In 1888 he was attempting to repeat some relevant graft experiments, intended to support pangenesis and, at the same time, to undermine Weismann's theory (Romanes to Dyer, 27/Dec./88, in: Romanes, 1896, p. 213; see also Romanes to Francis Darwin, 20/Jan./89, in: Romanes, 1896, pp. 216-217).

Toward the end of the 19th century, emphasis in the idea of use-inheritance was associated with the so-called "Neo-Lamarckian" school. Did Romanes include himself among Neo-Lamarckians? No, because "by Neo-Lamarckian school we understand all those naturalists who assign any higher importance to the Lamarckian factors than was assigned to them by Darwin" (Romanes, 1892-1897, vol. 2, p. 14). Of course, Romanes did not include himself in this group, because he was, in his own opinion, one of the few naturalists who correctly understood and accepted Darwin's view on "Lamarckian factors".

Sometimes, however, it seems that Romanes preferred Francis Galton's "stirp" theory of heredity instead Darwin's pangenesis:

> It is now close upon twenty years [Romanes wrote in 1893] that I accepted the substance of this theory under the name of stirp; and since that time the question as to the inheritance of acquired characters remains exactly where it was. No new facts, and no new considerations of much importance, have been forthcoming to assist us in answering it. Therefore, as already stated in the Preface, I intend to deal with this question hereafter as a question *per se*, or one which is not specially associated with the labours of Professor Weismann. (Romanes, 1896, pp. 170-171)

At another place, Romanes wrote:

> [...] I was myself one of the first evolutionists who called in question the Lamarckian factors; and ever since the publication of Galton's theory of heredity at about the same time, I have felt that in regard to its main principles – or those in which it agrees with Weismann's – it is probably the true one. (Romanes, 1896, p. 108)

Notice that by calling the attention of the readers to the similarity between some parts of the theory of germplasm and Galton's stirp theory, Romanes was also undermining any claims for Weismann's originality. However, instead of contrasting Galton and Darwin, Romanes chose to use both together against Weismann:

> Hence my object throughout has been to display, a sharply as possible, the contrast that is presented between the brass and the clay in the colossal figure which Weismann has constructed. Hence, also, my emphatic dissent from his theory of evolution does not prevent me from sincerely appreciating the great value which attaches to his theory of heredity. And although I have not hesitated to say that this theory is, in my opinion, incomplete; that it presents not a few manifest inconsistencies, and even logical contradictions; that the facts on which it is founded have always been facts of general knowledge; that in all its main features it was present to the mind of Darwin, and distinctly formulated by Galton; that in so far as it has been constituted the basis of a more general theory of organic evolution, it has clearly proved a failure: – such considerations in no wise diminish my cordial recognition of the services which its distinguished author has rendered to science by his speculations upon these topics. (Romanes, 1896, p. 115)

As shown above, Darwin's hypothesis of pangenesis had been severely criticized for being highly speculative. Romanes used the same charge against Weismann's theory of germplasm:

> [...] I confess to a serious doubt whether it [Weismann's theory] has not been permitted to enjoy an undue amount of liberty. If only they can be laced together by a thread of logical connection, hypotheses are added to hypotheses in such profusion as we are acquainted with in the works of metaphysicians, but which has rarely been approached in those of naturalists. The whole mechanism of heredity has been now planned out in such minuteness of detail and assurance of accuracy, that in reading the account one is reminded of that which is given by Dante of the topography of Inferno. For not only is the "sphere" of germ-plasm

now composed of nine circles. (molecules, biophores, determinants, ids, idants, idio-plasm, somatic-idioplasm, morpho-plasm, apical-plasm), but in most of these regions our guide is able to show us such strange and interesting phenomena, that we return to the fields of science with a sense of having been indeed in some other world. (Romanes, 1896, p. 118)

After showing that Weismann had profoundly altered several of the main assumptions of his former theory, Romanes remarked:

> 5. In my opinion it only remains for him to withdraw the last remnant of his theory of evolution by canceling his modified and even less tenable views on amphimixis, in order to give us a theory of heredity which is at once logically intact and biologically probable.
> 6. The theory of germ-plasm would then resemble that of stirp in all points of fundamental importance, save that while the latter leaves the question open as to whether acquired characters are ever inherited in any degree, the former would dogmatically close it, chiefly on the grounds which I have considered in Appendix II. It seems to me that in the present state of our knowledge it is more prudent to follow Galton in suspending our judgement with regard to this question, until time shall have been allowed for answering it by the inductive methods of observation and experiment. (Romanes, 1896, p. 170)

So, according to Romanes, Galton had proposed everything that was acceptable in Weismann's theory many years before. Other aspects of Weismann's theory were either wrong or unfounded.

Inheritance of acquired characters

In 1890 Romanes delivered his last course of lectures in Edinburgh. In that same year he accepted John Burton-Sanderson's invitation to work at Oxford (Romanes, 1896, pp. 260, 271). He moved from London to Oxford in May 1890, becoming a member of the University and a fellow of Christ Church College.

Romanes was now 42 years old. For the first time in his life he had at his disposal well equipped laboratories and assistants, providing full facilities for scientific research.

Romanes planned two main lines of experimental investigation. The first, that he had already began a few years before, was an attempt to provide an empirical foundation for the hypothesis of physiological selection. The second one was searching for confirmation of inheritance of acquired characters.

The question of reality or otherwise of the inheritance of acquired characters had no bearing on physiological selection. It was of the utmost strategical importance, however, because Wallace and Weismann denied that such a phenomenon could exist. If Romanes could provide a sound experimental foundation for the inheritance of acquired characters, he could completely overthrow the theories of the Neo-Darwinians. In a letter to his brother, Romanes told him about the relevance of those experiments:

> This is the most important question that has been raised in biology since I can remember, and one proof of an inherited *mutilation* would settle the matter against Weismann's theory. I am therefore also trying the mutilation of caterpillars at the Zoo, in the hope that a mutilation during what is virtually an embryonic period of life will be most likely to be transmitted, seeing that *congenital* variations are so readily transmissible, and that these are changes of a pre-embryonic kind. (Romanes to his brother James, undated letter [1890] in: Romanes, 1896, p. 245)

Romanes' wife also witnessed that those experiments were of the utmost importance for his husband:

> He devised many experiments to test that theory, experiments which have a pathetic interest for those who love him, for they

occupied his mind up to the very day of his death. (Romanes, 1896, p. 243)

The inheritance of acquired characters was one of the main subjects of the second volume of *Darwin, and after Darwin*. It had the sub-title: "Post-Darwinian questions – heredity and utility". The Preface clearly shows that in this volume Romanes intended to direct his weapons toward two main targets: Weismann's and Wallace's ideas. In the whole volume, one can find a remarkably large number of references to Wallace and Weismann. Their names appear in the book much more often than that of any other author – except Darwin, of course (see the Index of Romanes, 1892-1897, vol. 2, pp. 339-344).

> As regards Heredity, I have restricted the discussion almost exclusively to Professor Weismann's views, partly because he is at present by far the most important writer upon this subject, and partly because his views with regard to it raise with most distinctness the issue which lies at the base of all Post-Darwinian speculation touching this subject – the issue as to the inheritance or non-inheritance of acquired characters. (Romanes, 1892-1897, vol. 2, p. v)

The primary aim of the second volume of *Darwin, and after Darwin* was to discuss the "doubtful or erroneous" views of "the most eminent of Post-Darwinian writers".

> One more remark. It is a misfortune attending the aim and scope of Part II that they bring me into frequent discord with one or other of the most eminent of Post-Darwinian writers – especially with Mr. Wallace. But such is the case only because the subject-matter of this volume is avowedly restricted to debatable topics, and because I choose those naturalists who are deservedly held in most esteem to act spokesmen on behalf of such Post-Darwinian views as appear to me doubtful or erroneous. (Romanes, 1892-1897, vol. 2, p. vi)

The second volume was not intended to be read by general readers: "On the contrary, I have had in view a special class of readers; and, although I have tried not altogether to sacrifice the more general class, I shall desire it to be understood that I am there appealing to naturalists who are specialists in Darwinism" (Romanes, 1892-1897, vol. 1, p. 11).

First of all, in the 'Introduction' of this volume, Romanes attempted to establish what he regarded as Darwin's mature opinion on the several causes of organic evolution. He presented several citations of Darwin's work, showing his acceptance of "Lamarckian factors". He quoted various relevant texts from Darwin's books, such as the following one:

> A horse is trained to certain paces, and the colt inherits similar consensual movements. The domesticated rabbit becomes tame from close confinement; the dog, intelligent from associating with man; the retriever is taught to fetch and carry; and these mental endowments and bodily powers are all inherited. (Darwin, 1875, vol. 2, p. 367)

Romanes also recalled that the inheritance of acquired characters was an essential part of the hypothesis of pangenesis.

> Finally, it must not be forgotten that Darwin's acceptance of the theory of use-inheritance was vitally essential to his theory of Pangenesis – that "beloved child" over which he had "thought so much as to have lost all power of judging it". (Romanes, 1892-1897, vol. 2, p. 11)

Romanes fully reproduced the famous paragraph of the 'Conclusion' of the *Origin of species*, where Darwin clearly stated that he regarded natural selection as "the main, but not the exclusive means of modification". Romanes remarked: "In the whole range of Darwin's writing there cannot be found a passage so strongly worded as this" (Romanes, 1892-1897, vol. 2, p. 5).

> [...] and seeing that since the death of Darwin a large number of naturalists have gone over to the side of Wallace, it seems desirable here to state categorically what these other or sequent points of difference are. (Romanes, 1892-1897, vol. 2, p. 5)

Romanes contrasted Wallace's to Darwin's view in the following table (Romanes, 1892-1897, vol. 2, p. 6):

The theory of Natural Selection according to Darwin	*The theory of Natural Selection according to Wallace*
Natural Selection has been the main means of modification, not excepting the case of Man. (a) Therefore it is a question of evidence whether the Lamarckian factors have co-operated.	Natural Selection has been the sole means of modification, excepting the case of Man. (a) Therefore it is antecedently impossible that the Lamarckian factors can have co-operated.

(b) Neither all species, nor, *a fortiori*, all specific characters, have been due to natural selection.	(b) Not only species, but all specific characters, must necessarily have been due to natural selection.
(c) Thus the principle of Utility is not of universal application, even where species are concerned.	(c) Thus the principle of Utility must necessarily be universal application, where species are concerned.
(d) Thus, also, the suggestion as to Sexual Selection, or any other supplementary cause of modification, may be entertained; and, as in the case of the Lamarckian factors, it is a question of evidence whether, or how far, they have co-operated.	(d) Thus, also, the suggestion as to Sexual Selection, or of any other supplementary cause of modification, must be ruled out; and, as in the case of the Lamarckian factors, their co-operation deemed impossible.
(e) No detriment arises to the theory of natural selection as a theory of the origin of species by entertaining the possibility, or the probability, of supplementary factors.	(e) The possibility – and, *a fortiori*, the probability – of any supplementary factors cannot be entertained without serious detriment to the theory of natural selection, as a theory of the origin of species.
(f) Cross-sterility in species cannot possibly be due to natural selection.	(f) Cross-sterility in species is probably due to natural selection.

Romanes admitted that sometimes Wallace had not been that explicit concerning his points of disagreement with Darwin, but remarked: "[...] I am here taking Mr. Wallace as representative of the Neo-Darwinian school, one or other prominent member of which has given emphatic expression to each of the above propositions" (Romanes, 1892-1897, vol. 2, p. 7).

> It may now be added, that the longer he [Darwin] lived, and the more he pondered these points, the less exclusive was the *rôle* which he assigned to natural selection, and the more importance did he attribute to the supplementary factors above named. This admits of being easily demonstrated by comparing successive editions of his works; a method adopted by Mr. Herbert Spencer in his essay on the *Factors of Organic Evolution*. (Romanes, 1892-1897, vol. 2, p. 8)

Notice that although Romanes did not agree with Herbert Spencer (and criticized him in the first volume of *Darwin, and after Darwin*), he used his support, whenever that was useful to him.

Why was it necessary to contrast Darwin's to Wallace's views? According to Romanes, the main reason was not because they were different views, but because Wallace and his followers called themselves Darwinians:

> My object in thus clearly defining Darwin's attitude regarding these sundry points is twofold.
>
> In the first place, with regard to merely historical accuracy, it appears to me undesirable that naturalists should endeavour to hide certain parts of Darwin's teaching, and give undue prominence to others. In the second place, it appears to me still more undesirable that this should be done – as it usually is done – for the purpose of making it appear that Darwin's teaching did not really differ very much from that of Wallace and Weismann on the important points in question. I myself believe that Darwin's judgement with regard to all these points will eventually prove more sound and accurate than that of any of the recent would-be improvers upon his system [...]. Yet the new school of evolutionists, to which allusion has now so frequently been made, speak of their own modifications of Darwin's teaching as "pure Darwinism", in contradistinction to what they call "Lamarckism". [...] Now, of course, there is no reason why any one should not hold these or any other opinions to which his own independent study of natural science may lead him; but it appears to me that there is the very strongest reason why any one who deviates from the carefully formed opinions of such a man as Darwin, should above all things be careful to be absolutely fair in his representation of them; he should be scrupulously jealous, so to speak, of not letting it appear that he is unjustifiably throwing over his own opinions the authority of Darwin's name. (Romanes, 1892-1897, vol. 2, pp. 9-10)

So, Romanes argued that the Neo-Darwinians had no right to call themselves followers of Darwin. Besides that, he accused them of denying to others, who closely followed Darwin, the name of Darwinians:

> But in the present case, as we have seen, not only do the Neo-Darwinians strain the teachings of Darwin; they positively reverse those teachings – representing as anti-Darwinians the whole of one side of Darwin's system, and calling those who continue to

> accept that system in its entirety by the name "Lamarckians". (Romanes, 1892-1897, vol. 2, p. 10)
>
> Those biologists who of late years have been led by Weismann to adopt the opinions of Wallace, represent as anti-Darwinian the opinions of other biologists who still adhere to the unadulterated doctrines of Darwin. (Romanes, 1892-1897, vol. 2, p. 12)
>
> Yet so greatly have some of the Neo-Darwinians misunderstood the teachings of Darwin that they represent as "Darwinian heresy" any suggestion in the way of factors "supplementary to" or "co-operative with" natural selection. Of course, if these naturalists were to avow themselves followers of Wallace, instead of followers of Darwin, they would be perfectly justified in repudiating any such suggestion as, *ipso facto*, heretical. But, as we have now seen, through all his life Darwin differed from Wallace with regard to this very point [...]. (Romanes, 1892-1897, vol. 2, p. 11)
>
> Weismann's *Essay on Heredity*. (which argue that natural selection is the only possible cause of adaptive modification) and Wallace's work on *Darwinism*. (which in all the respects where any charge of "heresy" is concerned directly contradicts the doctrine of Darwin) – these are the writings which are now habitually represented by the Neo-Darwinians as setting forth the views of Darwin in their "pure" form. (Romanes, 1892-1897, vol. 2, p. 12)
>
> But we may easily escape this confusion, if we remember that wherever in the writings of these naturalists there occur such phrases as "pure Darwinism" we are to understand pure *Walleceism*, or the pure theory of natural selection to the exclusion of any supplementary theory. Therefore it is that for the sake of clearness I coined, several years ago, the terms "Neo-Darwinian" and "Ultra-Darwinian" whereby to designate the school in question. (Romanes, 1892-1897, vol. 2, p. 12)

It seems that Romanes concocted the term "Neo-Darwinism" to convey the sense that Weismann's and Wallace's views were a changed and spurious imitation of Darwinism, in the same way that the neo-classicism of the 17th and 18th centuries was not equivalent to the Classical spirit, and as Neo-Platonism was not faithful to Plato.

Wallace and Weismann did not agree in all respects. Wallace did not accept sexual selection, while Weismann did. Weismann developed a complex theory of heredity, while Wallace did not. Wallace could not accept that man had developed from lower animals by natural causes, while Weismann did. There were several other points of disagreement. Romanes, however, chose to emphasize their points of similarity, and to stress their joint opposition to his own interpretation of Darwin's theory, in order to kill two birds with a single shot.

> Looking, then, to these serious differences between his own doctrine of evolution – both organic and mental – and that of Darwin, I cannot think that Mr. Wallace has chosen a suitable title for his book; because, in view of the points just mentioned, it is unquestionable that *Darwinism* differs more widely from the *Origin of Species* than does the *Origin of Species* from the writings of the Neo-Lamarckians. (Romanes, 1892-1897, vol. 2, p. 22)

According to Wallace, neither the body [49] nor the mind of mankind can be explained by natural selection or by any other natural cause, requiring therefore the intervention of some supernatural entity. Romanes discussed at great length those features of Wallace's theory (Romanes, 1892-1897, vol. 2, pp. 22-33), contrasting them to Darwin's views and arguing for the continuity between animals and man, and for a gradual development of man's peculiar capacities.

> It can scarcely be said that any one of these questions has arisen altogether *de novo* during this period; for glimmerings, more of less conspicuous, of all are to be met with in the writings of Darwin himself. Nevertheless it is no less true that only after his death have they been lighted up to the full blaze of active discussion. (Romanes, 1892-1897, vol. 2, pp. 35-36)

According to Romanes, Francis Galton was the first author to challenge the efficacy of the "Lamarckian factors" (inheritance of acquired characters), in his book *Theory of Heredity* (1875). It seems that this work strongly influenced Romanes:

> Lastly, I was myself led to doubt the Lamarckian factors still further back in the seventies, by having found a reason for questioning the main evidence which Mr. Darwin had adduced in their favour[50]. This doubt was greatly strengthened on reading, in the following year, Mr. Galton's *Theory of Heredity* just alluded to; and thereupon I commenced a prolonged course of experiments

---

[49] Wallace claimed that the feet, the hands, the brain, the voice and the naked skin of man could not be explained by natural selection.

[50] Romanes is here referring to his 1874 papers, published in *Nature* (Romanes, 1892-1897, vol. 2, p. 98).

upon the subject, the general nature of which will be stated in future chapters. (Romanes, 1892-1897, vol. 2, p. 40)

> For my own part, as stated in the *Examination* [*of Weismannism*], I have always been disposed to accept Mr. Galton's theory of Stirp in preference to that of Germ-plasm on this very ground – i.e. that it does not dogmatically exclude the possibility of an occasional inheritance of acquired characters in faint though cumulative degrees. (Romanes, 1892-1897, vol. 2, p. 42)

Romanes regarded both the evidence presented by Weismann against inheritance of acquired characters, and all evidence presented in support of that phenomenon, as far from demonstrative: "Therefore at present the question must remain for the most part a matter or opinion, based upon general reasoning as distinguished from special facts or crucial experiments. The evidence available on either side is presumptive, not demonstrative" (Romanes, 1892-1897, vol. 2, p. 57).

In this book, Romanes referred to his trials of producing graft-hybrids as experiments attempting to test the inheritance of acquired characters (Romanes, 1892-1897, vol. 2, pp. 142-144). That was not really their original aim: they were attempts to check the hypothesis of pangenesis.

In this book, as in other of his works, Romanes directly attacked several authors, while Darwin never did so – one can only find very mild and passing criticism of any author given by name, although, of course, he does criticize many *ideas*. However, Romanes wrote about Darwin's opinions as if he had himself directly criticized Wallace: "Mr. Darwin repudiated Mr. Wallace's doctrine touching the *necessary* utility of *all* specific characters" (Romanes, 1892-1897, vol. 2, p. 314).

The third and final volume of *Darwin, and after Darwin*, was published in 1897, three years after Romanes' death. This volume, as edited by Lloyd Morgan, was not a polemical book[51]. It presented the theory of physiological selection in a much clearer way than in the original 1886 paper. In this volume, contrasting to the former one, Wallace and Weismann were mentioned (and criticized) only a few times. Also, Romanes was wise enough to leave out of those pages

---

[51] Lloyd Morgan, the editor of volumes 2 and 3 of *Darwin, and after Darwin*, omitted "two long controversial Appendices" (Romanes, *Darwin, and after Darwin*, vol. 3, p. v).

anything that could be interpreted as an attack against Darwin. Given the aim of the present work, it will not be necessary to provide further information on this volume.

Romanes' illness

Romanes' health had never been excellent, but after his move to Oxford it was getting worse and worse. Romanes had frequent headaches that lowered his research capacity. In June 1892, shortly after the publication of *An examination of Weismannism*, Romanes lost the sight of one eye (Romanes, 1896, p. 300).

> About ten days ago I found myself partially blind in the right eye – the upper half of the field of vision being totally obliterated. [...] It seems probable that the impairment of vision will be permanent, and so prevent all operative work where any delicacy is required. [...] *Per contra*, this may prove a blessing in disguise, as it compels me to abstain from work for some considerable time to come, and I had been advised to this course on account of the headaches. (Romanes to his sister Charlotte, 18/June/92, in: Romanes, 1896, p. 302)

Romanes was greatly concerned that because of his illness it would be impossible to continue his experiments on the inheritance of acquired characters:

> My eye trouble prevents me from carrying on my experiments in heredity, except by deputy; this to me is most provoking, as they have been yielding very interesting results; and having now trained my hands for the performance of the more delicate among them, I am doubtful where I can find the deputy which I need. I mention this in case you should happen to know of any young physiologist who, possessing some operative skill, would care to join in the research. I am ordered six months' rest from any kind of intellectual work [...]. (Romanes to Huxley, 18/June/92, in: Romanes, 1896, p. 297)

After a few days, a second blind spot appeared. Romanes had a hypertension crisis and doctors thought that his life was threatened (Romanes, 1896, p. 303). For two years, his health was precarious.

> The one difficulty was to persuade him not to work, and this was almost impossible. He was almost feverishly anxious to finish his book, to work out experiments he had been planning [...]. (Romanes, 1896, p. 303)

Romanes' health improved in the following months, and he returned to work. He was trying to finish volumes 2 and 3 of *Darwin, and after Darwin*, and to continue his experimental researches. On the 11th July 1893, however, he has taken by a partial paralysis (hemiplegia). Romanes' wife wrote that "from that time the Shadow of Death was ever on him, and he knew it; from that July day he regarded himself as doomed" (Romanes, 1896, p. 335)

> Sometimes the longing to finish his work was too great to be borne, but generally he was calm, and always, even when he was most sad, he was gentle and patient, and willing to be amused. (Romanes, 1896, p. 336)

Although he was facing death, Romanes remained anxious to continue his work. He made arrangements for the publication of volumes 2 and 3 of *Darwin, and after Darwin*:

> [...] if he was not listening to reading or conversation, he would be planning experiments or pondering problems of theology, and ask by-and-by that his thoughts should be taken down from dictation, or that paper and pencil should be given him, or, worse than all, devising arrangements for finishing 'Darwin, and after Darwin'. He dictated some 'Thoughts on Things' in the very first days of his illness, and sent for Professor Lloyd Morgan, who came and received instructions about the unfinished books, instructions which he has carried out with unflagging diligence and never-failing kindness[52]. (Romanes, 1896, p. 337)

Romanes' greatest worry was that he regarded his work as incomplete. The theory of physiological selection had not been established, and he had not been able to win his battle against the Neo-Darwinians. He thought that he would succeed if he could continue his work for one more decade:

> Looking all the facts in the face, I do not expect to see another birthday, and therefore, like Job, am disposed to curse my first one. For I know that all my best work was to have been published in the next ten or fifteen years; and it is wretched to think of how much labour in the past will thus be wasted. (Romanes to Dyer, 18/Sept./93, in: Romanes, 1896, p. 342)

---

[52] The second and third volumes of *Darwin and after Darwin* were published posthumously (1895 and 1897) under the editorship of Romanes' friend Lloyd Morgan.

Even during the last months of his life (October 1893 to April 1894), Romanes was able to sustain a detailed discussion with George Henslow, who was proposing the concept of "self-adaptation" to account for evolution (Romanes, 1896, pp. 356-371). His main concern throughout this period was, however, Weismann's theory. In the beginning of 1893 Romanes was very ill and had been sent to Madeira Island by his physicians, but he kept in touch with the development of Weismann's theory:

> I have got Weismann's new book, 'The Germ-Plasm'. It is a much more finished performance than the 'Essays'. In fact, he has evidently been consulting botanists, reading up English literature on the subject, so he has anticipated nearly all the points of my long criticisms. This is a nuisance.
>
> *Per contra*, since coming here I have heard of no less than three additional cases of cats which have lost their tails afterwards having tailless kittens. I wish to goodness I had been more energetic in getting on with my experiments about this, so I have written to John to get me twelve kittens to meet me on my return. It would be a grand thing to knock down W.'s whole edifice with a cat's tail. (Romanes to his wife Ethel, 19/March/93, in: Romanes, 1896, p. 323)

Romanes was positively impressed by the gradual improvement of Weismann's theory, and as he read *The germ-plasm* he wrote to his wife:

> Here is an odd thing. I find that Weismann in his new book has discussed all the points raised by Spencer. So Spencer and I have been hammering away at things which W. has already written upon. (Romanes to his wife Ethel, 21/March/93, in: Romanes, 1896, p. 323)

> I have been busy with my answer to H. Spencer. H. S. is singularly behindhand with his information. In fact, it is melancholy to see how he fails to appreciate the strength of Weismann's position[53]. He does not even understand it, and the weakness of his criticism is such that he makes matters worse for his own position with regard to the inheritance of acquired characters – *i.e.* the

---

[53] In 1893 and 1894, there was a famous debate in the pages of the *Contemporary Review* between Weismann and Spencer on the possibility of use-inheritance and on the role of natural selection in evolution (Robinson, 1970, p. 237).

> foundation of his entire system of synthetic philosophy. (Romanes to his wife Ethel, 22/March/93, in: Romanes, 1896, p. 324)

Although Romanes had strongly attacked Weismann's work, he was convinced that the theory of the germplasm was a worthy scientific contribution, and he decided to invite Weismann to present a lecture to the Oxford University:

> I have asked W. if he will give the Romanes Lecture[54] some year. (Romanes to his wife Ethel, 22/March/93, in: Romanes, 1896, p. 324)

In April 1894 – a few weeks before his death – Romanes received a letter from Weismann accepting the invitation to deliver the Romanes Lecture (Romanes, 1896, p. 377).

> On May 3 came the third Romanes Lecture. It was given by Professor Weismann, and was a worthy successor to the two which had preceded it.
> Mr. Romanes was glad to meet Professor Weismann, and enjoyed the pleasant talk he and his distinguished opponent had in his house after the lecture. (Romanes, 1896, p. 378)

Although Romanes' sight was seriously impaired and he had locomotion difficulties, he kept trying to work up to the end: "He was often at the Museum, and he wrote frequently of the experiments he was devising, all bearing on Professor Weismann's theory; in these he was assisted by Dr. Leonard Hill" (Romanes, 1896, p. 378).

George John Romanes expired on the 23rd May 1894, when he was only 46 years old.

---

[54] In 1891 Romanes presented to the Oxford University an offer to found an annual lectureship. The University accepted his offer, and they were called "Romanes Lectures". During his lifetime, Romanes himself invited the speakers. The two first were Gladstone and Huxley. Weismann accepted Romanes' request, and gave the third Romanes Lecture. This series of lectures still exist nowadays.

Final remarks

As a result of his scientific work, "[...] Romanes proved to be one of the most brilliant of the second generation of British Darwinists" (Lesch, 1970, p. 517). All evidence, however, points out that Romanes was not satisfied with his achievement. He had entertained a higher ambition, and had to give it up due to his illness:

> With absolute resignation **he gave up all his ambitions, the old longing for distinction, for greater fame**, and yet he did not lose for one moment the old interest in his scientific work. (Romanes, 1896, p. 353; my emphasis)

I offer as a plausible interpretation of Romanes' behavior that after Darwin's death there was a struggle for recognition and leadership *among Darwinians*. Romanes attempted to become the topmost evolutionist, the heir of Darwin's mantle. All his professional strategies can be understood in the light of this interpretation of his life. Whether consciously or not, he made use of several tactics that could contribute to that aim:

1. He always wrote about Darwin in a most respectful way, and defended the Master against criticism, as was required from anyone who expected to be recognized as Darwin's scientific successor.
2. He attempted to show that his own interpretation of Darwinism was faithful to Darwin's ideas.
3. He criticized the interpretation of Darwinism proposed by other Darwinians (especially Wallace and Weismann) and attempted to show that Neo-Darwinism was incompatible with Darwin's original thought.
4. He attempted to complement the theory of natural selection, proposing a new theory that could answer to serious difficulties of Darwin's theory.
5. He tried to provide a solid empirical foundation for physiological selection and to obtain acceptance for his theory.
6. He made an effort to keep himself in evidence, by publications, lectures, and public controversies.

7. He endeavored to undermine the scientific work of the strongest contestants who were fighting for Darwin's mantle (the Neo-Darwinians) presenting arguments and trying to present empirical evidence against their views (especially as regards inheritance of acquired characters).
8. He tried to obtain support from key persons, whom he supported and did not criticize, in turn.

If this reconstruction of Romanes' strategy is correct, he had a strong professional program and had a good chance of being successful. Had his experimental studies been victorious and had he lived enough to continue his campaign, it is likely that Romanes could attain the leadership of the Darwinian group in the turn of the century.

References

[ANON]. Physiological selection and the origin of species. *The Times* (London) Aug 16: 8, 1886.

[ANON.]. George John Romanes. In memoriam. *The Monist*, **4** (4): 482, 1894.

BOWLER, Peter. *Evolution. The history of an idea.* Revised edition. Berkeley: University of California Press, 1989.

────── . *Charles Darwin: The man and his influence.* Cambridge: Cambridge University Press, 1990.

BUTLER, Samuel. *Luck, or cunning, as the main means of organic modification? An attempt to throw additional light upon Darwin's theory of natural selection.* London: A. C. Fifield, 1910.

DARWIN, Charles. Pangenesis. *Nature*, **3**: 502-503, 1871.

────── . *The origin of species by natural selection or the preservation of favoured races in the struggle for life.* 6th ed. London: John Murray, 1872.

────── . *The variation of animals and plants under domestication* 2nd ed. London: John Murray, 1875.

────── . *The autobiography of Charles Darwin.* Ed. Nora Barlow. London: Collins, 1948.

DARWIN, Francis (ed.). *The life and letters of Charles Darwin.* 3 vols. London: John Murray, 1887.

────── . *More letters of Charles Darwin.* 2 vols. New York: D. Appleton and Co., 1903.

FLANNERY, Michael A. *Alfred Russel Wallace: a rediscovered life.* Seattle: Discover Institute Press, 2011.

FORSDYKE, Donald R. The origin of species, revisited. *Queen's Quarterly*, **106** (1): 112-134, 1999.

────── . *Origin of Species revisited: a Victorian who anticipated modern developments in Darwin's theory.* Kingston: McGill-Queen's University Press, 2001.

────── . *Evolutionary bioinformatics.* New York: Springer, 2006.

———. George Romanes, William Bateson, and Darwin's 'weak point'. *Notes and Records of the Royal Society*, **64**: 139-154, 2010.

GALTON, Francis. Experiments in Pangenesis. *Proceedings of the Royal Society of London*, **19**: 1393-1411, 1871.

———. Pangenesis. *Nature*, **4**: 5, 1871.

LESCH, John E. The role of isolation in evolution: George J. Romanes and John T. Gulick. *Isis*, **66**: 483-503, 1975.

———. Romanes, George John. Vol. 11, pp. 516-20, in: GILLIESPIE, Charles Coulston (ed.). *Dictionary of Scientific Biography*. 16 vols. New York: Charles Scribner's Sons, 1970.

LEWES, George Henry. Mr. Darwin's hypotheses. *The Fortnightly Review*, **3**: 353-373, 611-628, 1868; **4**: 61-80, 492-509, 1868.

LYNCH, John M. [Review] The Origin of Species Revisited. *Journal of the History of Biology*, **37**: 211-212, 2004.

MARCHANT, James (ed.). *Alfred Russel Wallace – letters and reminiscences*. London: Cassell and Co., 1916. 2 vols.

MARTINS, Roberto de Andrade. George John Romanes e a teoria da seleção fisiológica. *Episteme*, **11** (24): 197-208, jul./dez. 2006.

MAYR, Ernst. *The growth of biological thought: diversity, evolution, and inheritance*. Cambridge, Harvard University Press, 1982.

MELDOLA, Raphael. Physiological selection and the origin of species. *Nature*, **34**: 384, 26 August 1886.

MORRIS, William (ed.). *The heritage illustrated dictionary of the English language*. Boston: American Heritage, 1975.

MÜLLER, Friedrich Max. On thought and language. A lecture delivered before the Philosophical Society of Glasgow, on Jan. 21, 1891. *The Monist*, **1** (4): 572-589, 1891.

PLEINS, J. David. *In praise of Darwin. George Romanes and the evolution of a Darwinian believer*. New York: Bloomsbury, 2014.

RABY, Peter. *Alfred Russel Wallace: a life*. London: Pimlico, 2002.

ROBINSON, Gloria. Weismann, August Freidrich Leopold. Vol. 14, pp. 232-239, in: GILLIESPIE, Charles Coulston (ed.). *Dictionary of Scientific Biography*. 16 vols. New York: Charles Scribner's Sons, 1970.

ROMANES, Ethel. *The life and letters of George John Romanes*. London: Longmans, Green, and Co., 1896.

ROMANES, George John. Permanent variation of colour in fish. *Nature*, **8**: 101, 1873.

———. Disuse as a reducing cause in species. *Nature*, **9**: 361, 440; **10**: 164, 1874.

———. Preliminary observations on the locomotor system of medusae (Croonian Lecture). *Philosophical Transactions of the Royal Society*, **166**: 269-313, 1876.

———. Further observations on the locomotor system of medusae. *Philosophical Transactions of the Royal Society*, **167**: 659-752, 1877.

———. Concluding observations on the locomotor system of medusae. *Philosophical Transactions of the Royal Society*, **171**: 161-202, 1880.

———. The scientific evidence of organic evolution. *Fortnightly Review*, **36**: 739-758, 1881.

———. *The scientific evidences of organic evolution*. London, Macmillan and Co., 1882.

———. *Animal intelligence*. New York: D. Appleton and Co., 1883.

———. *Mental evolution in animals*. New York: D. Appleton and Co., 1884.

———. *Jelly-fish, star-fish, and sea urchins, being a research into primitive nervous systems*. London: Kegan Paul, Trench & Co., 1885.

———. Physiological selection: an additional suggestion on the origin of species. *Journal of the Linnean Society, Zoology*, **19**: 337-411, 1886.

———. The factors of organic evolution. *Nature*, **35**: 362-364, 1886-1887; **36**: 401-407, 1887.

———. Physiological selection. *Nineteenth Century*, **21**: 59-80, 1887.

———. *Mental evolution in man, origin of human faculty*. New York: D. Appleton and Co., 1889.

———. Wallace on *Darwinism*. *Contemporary Review*, **56**: 244-258, 1889.

———. Before and after Darwin. *Nature*, **41**: 524-525, 1889-1890.

———. Weismann's theory of heredity. *Contemporary Review*, **57**: 686-699, 1890. Reproduced in: *Annual Report of the Board of Regents of the Smithsonian Institution*, 433-446, 1890.

———. Are the effects of use and disuse inherited? *Nature*, **43**: 217-220, 1890-1891.

———. Mr. A. R. Wallace on physiological selection. *Monist*, **1**: 1-20, 1890-1891.

———. *Darwinism illustrated; wood-engravings explanatory of the theory of evolution*. Chicago: The Open Court Publishing Company, 1892.

———. Mr. Herbert Spencer on 'Natural selection'. *Contemporary Review*, **63**: 499-517, 1893.

———. The Spencer-Weismann controversy. *Contemporary Review*, **64**: 50-53, 1893.

———. A note on Panmixia. *Contemporary Review*, **64**: 611-612, 1893.

———. *An examination of Weismannism*. Chicago: Open Court, 1896.

———. *Darwin, and after Darwin*. 3 vols. Chicago: Open Court, 1892-1897.

ROMANES, George John & EWART, James Cossar. Observations on the locomotor system of echinodermata. *Philosophical Transactions of the Royal Society*, **172**: 829-885, 1881.

SLOTTEN, Ross A. *The heretic in Darwin's court: the life of Alfred Russel Wallace*. New York: Columbia University Press, 2012.

SCHWARTZ, Joel S. Darwin, Wallace, and the *Descent of man*. *Journal of the History of Biology*, **17**: 271-289, 1984.

———. George John Romanes's defense of Darwinism: the correspondence of Charles Darwin and his chief disciple. *Journal of the History of Biology*, **28**: 281-316, 1995.

———. Out from Darwin's Shadow: George John Romanes's efforts to popularize science in "Nineteenth Century" and other Victorian periodicals. *Victorian Periodicals Review*, **35** (2): 133-159, 2002.

———. *Darwin's disciple: George John Romanes, a life in letters*. Philadelphia: Lightning Rod Press / American Philosophical Society, 2010.

SPENCER, Herbert. *The facts of organic evolution*. New York: D. Appleton, 1887.

———. The inadequacy of natural selection. *Contemporary Review*, **63**: 153-166, 439-456, 1893.

———. *The inadequacy of 'natural selection'*. New York: D. Appleton, 1893.

VORZIMMER, Peter. Charles Darwin and blending inheritance. *Isis*, **54**: 371-390, 1963.

WALLACE, Alfred Russel. Review of 'Principles of Geology' by C. Lyell. *Quarterly Review*, **126**: 187-205, 1869.

―――― . Romanes *versus* Darwin: an episode in the history of evolution theory. *Fortnightly Review*, **46**: 300-316, 1886.

―――― . *Darwinism: an exposition of the theory of natural selection, with some of its applications*. London: Macmillan, 1889.

WEISMANN, August. *Essays upon heredity and kindred biological problems*. Trans. Edward B. Poulton, Selmar Schönland and Arthur E. Shipley. Oxford: Clarendon Press, 1889.

―――― . *The germ-plasm. A theory of heredity*. Trans. Newton W. Parker, Harriet Rönnfeldt. New York: Charles Scribner's Sons, 1893.

YOUNG, David. *The discovery of evolution*. Cambridge: Cambridge University Press, 1962.

Second part: Physiological selection

This second part of the book contains Romanes' 1886 article on physiological selection, complemented by several footnotes providing additional information and pointing out some particularly strong or weak points of the paper. All notes by Roberto de Andrade Martins are marked as [RAM]. Any footnotes without this mark belong to Romanes' original article. The page divisions of the original paper are marked in the text – for instance, [p. 391]. The author is grateful to the Linnean Society for permission to reproduce the full text of the article.

Physiological Selection; an Additional Suggestion on the Origin of Species[+]

By GEORGE J. ROMANES, M.A., LL.D., F.R.S., F.L.S.

[Read 6th May, 1886]

Introduction

There can be no one to whom I yield in my veneration for the late Mr. Darwin, or in my appreciation of his work. But for this very reason I feel that in now venturing to adopt in some measure an attitude of criticism towards that work[55], a few words are needed to show that I have not done so hastily, or without due premeditation.

It is now fifteen years since I became a close student of Darwinism, and during the greater part of that time I have had the privilege of discussing the whole philosophy of Evolution with Mr. Darwin himself. In the result I have found it impossible to entertain a doubt, either upon Evolution as a fact, or upon Natural Selection as a method. But during all these years it has seemed to me that there are certain weak points in the otherwise unassailable defences with which Mr. Darwin has fortified his citadel, or in the evidences with which he has surrounded his theory of natural selection[56]. And the more I have thought upon these points, the greater has seemed the difficulty which they present; until at last I became satisfied that some cause, or

---

[+] *The Journal of the Linnean Society. Zoology* **19**: 337-411, 1886. Published July 23rd, 1886.

[55] Notice that Romanes here explicitly states that this paper presents a criticism of Darwin's work. His attitude produced a negative reaction from several of his contemporaries. [RAM]

[56] Although Romanes disagrees with Darwin concerning the production of new species and points out "certain weak points", notice that he takes advantage of his close connection with Darwin and that he also claims that there are some points of the theory of evolution that cannot be doubted. [RAM]

causes, must have been at work in the production of species other than that of natural selection, and yet of an equally general kind[57].

While drifting into this position of scepticism with regard to natural selection as in itself a full explanation of the origin of species, it was to me a satisfaction to find that other evolutionists, including Mr. Darwin himself, were travelling the same way[58]. And since Mr. Darwin's death the tide of opinion continues to flow in this direction; so that at the present time it would be impossible to find any working naturalist who supposes that survival of the fittest is competent to explain all the phenomena of species-formation; while on the side of general reasoning we need not go further than the current issue of the 'Nineteenth Century' to meet with a systematic statement of this view by the highest living authority upon the philosophy of evolution[59]. Therefore, [p. 338] in now adopting an attitude of criticism towards certain portions of Mr. Darwin's work, I cannot feel that I am turning traitor to the cause of Darwinism[60]. On the contrary, I hope thus to remove certain difficulties in the way of Darwinian teaching; and I well know that Mr. Darwin himself would have been the first to welcome my attempt at suggesting another factor in the formation of species, which, although quite independent of natural selection, is in no way opposed to natural selection, and may therefore be regarded as a factor supplementary to natural selection[61].

---

[57] That is, Romanes believed that his own additional theory of "physiological selection" is as general (and perhaps as important) as that of natural selection. [RAM]

[58] Here, Romanes claimed that Darwin himself had doubts concerning the all-sufficiency of natural selection. [RAM]

[59] Although Romanes did not provide an explicit reference here, he was certainly referring to two papers by Herbert Spencer that appeared in the April and May 1886 issues of *The Nineteenth Century*: SPENCER, Herbert. The factors of organic evolution. *The Nineteenth Century*, **19**: 570-589; 749-770, 1886. This essay was reprinted in book form in the next year, with some additions: SPENCER, Herbert. *The factors of organic evolution*. London: Williams and Norgate, 1887. Spencer accepted natural section as one of the causes of evolution but he claimed that this process cannot explain all the features of evolution. [RAM]

[60] Some contemporaries did claim that Romanes became a traitor to Darwin's memory. [RAM]

[61] Darwin knew Romanes' hypothesis of "physiological selection" but he did not accept it. Hence, Romanes' suggestion that Darwin would accept this supplementary factor is false, and is just a rhetorical stratagem. [RAM]

Difficulties against Natural Selection as a Theory of the Origin of Species

The cardinal difficulties in the way of natural selection, considered as a theory of the origin of species, are three in number[62]:

1st. The difference between natural species and domesticated varieties in respect of fertility.

Mr. Darwin himself allows that this difference cannot be explained by natural selection; and indeed proves very clearly, as well as very candidly, that it must be due to causes hitherto undetected. As we shall presently find, he treats this difficulty at greater length and with more elaboration than any other; but, as we shall also find, entirely fails to overcome it[63]. Now, seeing of how much importance to any theory on the origin of species is the great and general fact of sterility between species, I need not wait to show how heavily we must here discount the theory of natural selection, considered as a theory to explain the transmutation of species.

2nd. Another fact of almost equal generality is that the features, even other than sterility *inter se*, which serve to distinguish allied species, are frequently, if not usually, of a kind with which natural selection can have had nothing whatever to do; for distinctions of specific value frequently have reference to structures which are without any utilitarian significance . It is not until we advance to the more important distinctions between genera, families, and orders that we begin to find, on any large or general scale, unmistakable evidence of utilitarian meaning.

This difficulty, as I have MS evidence to show[64], was first perceived by Mr. Darwin himself; it was afterwards presented in a formidable shape by the German paleontologist Bronn[65], and subsequently by Broca, Nägeli, and sundry lesser writers as regards

---

[62] Romanes strategically mentions only the difficulties which he assumes can be solved by his own theory. There were many other points of Darwin's theory criticized by contemporary authors. [RAM]

[63] It is likely that Romanes was not willing to condemn Darwin directly, but the wording he used implied that Darwin tried but failed to solve this difficulty. [RAM]

[64] Because of his intimate acquaintance with Darwin, Romanes had access to his manuscripts, as claimed here. [RAM]

[65] Concerning Heinrich Georg Bronn's work, see JUNKER, Thomas. Heinrich Georg Bronn und die Entstehung der Arten. *Sudhoffs Archiv für Geschichte der Medizin und der Naturwissenschaften*, 75:180-208, 1991.

[p. 339] both plants and animals. To all these criticisms Darwin replies in the last editions of his works[*], with what degree of success I will presently consider.

3rd. The third and last difficulty which I have to mention consists in the swamping influence upon an incipient variety of free intercrossing. This difficulty was first prominently announced in an anonymous essay by the late Professor Fleeming Jenkin [66] of Edinburgh, published in the 'North British Review' for 1867[†]. If to

---

[*] See 'Origin of Species,' ed. 6, pp. 156-157 and 169-176. 'Variation' &c. ii. pp. 211-219. And as to Instincts, ' Mental Evolution in Animals,' pp. 378-379.

[66] [JENKIN, Fleeming]. [Review of] The origin of species. *The North British Review*, **46**: 277-318, June 1867. For an analysis of Jenkin's review, see MORRIS, Susan W. Fleeming Jenkin and The Origin of Species: a reassessment. *The British Journal for the History of Science*, 27: 313-343, 1994. Jenkin claimed that any advantageous mutations which might arise in a species would be quickly diluted out of any species after just a few generations, because of the swamping effects of blending inheritance. In the next footnote, Romanes stated that Darwin was unable to answer to this criticism. Concerning the cogency of Jenkin's argument, see BULMER, Michael. Did Jenkin's swamping argument invalidate Darwin's theory of natural selection? *The British Journal for the History of Science*, **37**: 281-297, 2004. [RAM]

[†] This article is in all respects a highly remarkable one, and, for the space it covers, presents more searching and effective criticism of Mr. Darwin's theory than any other essay with which I am acquainted. With regard to this particular difficulty from the swamping effects of intercrossing, the criticism is especially cogent, and, so far as I know, is the only criticism of importance which Mr. Darwin has not expressly answered. Without reproducing all the numerical calculations wherewith the author sustains this criticism, it will here be enough to quote one of his illustrations:

"Suppose a white man to have been wrecked on an island inhabited by negroes, and to have established himself in friendly relations with a powerful tribe whose customs he has learnt. Suppose him to possess the physical strength, energy, and ability of a dominant white race, and let the food and climate of the island suit his constitution; grant him every advantage which can conceive a white to possess over the native; concede that in the struggle for existence his chance of a long life will be much superior to that of the native chiefs. Yet from all these admissions there does not follow the conclusion that after a limited or unlimited number of generations the inhabitants of the island will be white. Our shipwrecked hero would probably become king; he would kill a great many blacks in the struggle for existence; he would have a great many wives and children, while many of his subjects would live and die as bachelors; an insurance company would accept his life at perhaps one tenth of the premium which they would exact from the most favoured of the negroes. Our white's qualities would certainly tend very much to preserve him to a good old age; and yet he would not suffice in any number of generations to turn his subjects' descendants white. It may be said that the white colour is not the cause of the superiority. True; but

this difficulty we add the consideration adduced [p. 340] by this author, and afterwards in a more elaborate form by Professor Mivart[67], as to the improbability of a variation being from the first of sufficient utility to come under the influence of natural selection, I feel it impossible to doubt that a most formidable opposition is presented. For even if, for the sake of argument, we waive Professor Mivart's objection as to the probable inutility of many incipient variations which afterwards, or in a higher degree of perfection, begin to become useful, even if we waive this objection and assume that all useful variations are useful from the first moment of variation, still we have to meet the difficulty from the swamping effects of free intercrossing on the incipient variation, however useful.

Here then we have three great obstructions in the road of natural selection, considered as an explanation of the origin of species. For the sake of brevity I will hereafter allude to these difficulties as those relating to sterility, to inutility, and to intercrossing. Let us now consider how these difficulties have been dealt with in the later editions of Mr. Darwin's works.

---

it may be used simply to bring before the senses the way in which qualities belonging to one individual in a large number must be gradually obliterated. In the first generation there will be some dozens of intelligent young mulattoes, much superior in average intelligence to the negroes. We might expect the throne for some generations to be occupied by a more or less yellow king; but can any one believe that the whole island will gradually acquire a white or even a yellow population, or that the islanders would acquire the energy, courage, ingenuity, patience, self-control, endurance, in virtue of which qualities our hero killed so many of their ancestors, and begot so many children; those qualities, in fact, which the struggle for existence would select, if it could select anything?

"Here is a case in which a variety was introduced with far greater advantages than any sport ever heard of, advantages tending to its preservation, and yet powerless to perpetuate the new variety."

[67] Mivart first presented his criticism of Darwin's theory in a series of three papers: MIVART, St. George Jackson. Difficulties of the theory of natural selection. *The Month*, **11**: 35–53; 134–153; 274–289, 1869. His views were also presented in his famous book: MIVART, St. George Jackson. *On the genesis of species*. New York: D. Appleton and Co., 1871, and several further papers. For an analysis of the controversy between Mivart and Darwin, see REGNER, Anna Carolina. Charles Darwin versus George Mivart. Pp. 51-75, in: EEMEREN, Frans Hendrik; GARSSEN, Bart (eds.). *Controversy and confrontation: relating controversy analysis with argumentation theory*. Amsterdam: John Benjamins Publishing, 2008. [RAM]

Sterility between Species

Founding his argument for natural selection upon the basis furnished by the known effects of artificial selection, Mr. Darwin had to meet the question why it is that the supposed products of the former, differ from the known products of the latter, in being so much more sterile *inter se*; or, in other words, why it is that natural species differ so conspicuously from artificial varieties in respect of mutual fertility. In order to meet this question, Mr. Darwin adduced a variety of considerations, each of which he substantiated by so large an accumulation of facts, that, as I have already observed, his discussion of the question as a whole is one of the most laboured portions of all his laborious work. From which we may perceive how fully Mr. Darwin recognized the formidable nature of this difficulty. I will now summarize the considerations whereby be sought to overcome it. And this I can do most briefly by arranging them in an order of my own. [p. 341]

In the first place, differences of type in nature are by naturalists classified as differences of species, principally because they are found to be mutually sterile. Thus it is but circular reasoning to argue that all natural species are shown by nature herself to differ from artificial varieties in presenting this peculiarity of mutual sterility; for it is mainly in virtue of presenting this peculiarity that they have been classified as species. The real question, therefore, that stands to be considered is simply this: Why should the modifications of organic types supposed to have been produced by natural selection have so frequently and generally led to mutual sterility, when even greater modifications of such types known to have been produced by artificial selection continue to be mutually fertile?

In the next place, the distinction in question is not absolute. On the one hand, some few domesticated varieties, when crossed with one another, exhibit a more or less marked degree of sterility; and, on the other hand, a large number of wild species, when crossed with one another, exhibit fertility, and this in all degrees. So that the distinction between natural species and artificial varieties in respect of fertility is, as a matter of fact, not absolute, but breaks down in both its parts.

Nevertheless, although this distinction is not absolute, it is undoubtedly, and as a general rule, valid. That is to say, it is unusual or exceptional to find complete fertility between natural species, and it is still more so to find even partial sterility between artificial varieties. Therefore, notwithstanding his success in showing that there is no absolute distinction between species and varieties in this respect, Mr. Darwin plainly perceived that there still remained a relative distinction of a most general and important kind. In order to mitigate the severity of this distinction, be furnished elaborate proof of the following facts.

1st. That with natural species the cause of sterility lies exclusively in differences of the sexual system.

2nd. That the conditions of life which occur under domestication tend to enhance fertility, and this to such an extent as to render the domesticated descendants of mutually sterile species mutually fertile, as in the case of our domesticated dogs.

Now, these two facts undoubtedly help to explain why the great changes of organic types produced by artificial selection have not resulted in superinducing mutual sterility; but they do not appear to throw any light at all on the question, why it is [p. 342] that smaller changes of organic type, when produced by natural selection and now known as species, should so generally be attended with this result? Or, as Mr. Darwin himself expresses it, "the real difficulty in our present subject is not, as it appears to me, why domestic varieties have not become mutually infertile when crossed, but why this has so generally occurred with natural varieties, as soon as they have been permanently modified in a sufficient degree to take rank as species."

Here, then, we have the core of the problem; and it is just here that Mr. Darwin's explanations fail. For he candidly says, "We are far from precisely knowing the cause;" and the only suggestion he adduces to account for the fact is, that varieties occurring under nature "will have been exposed during long periods of time to more uniform conditions than have domesticated varieties; and this may well make a wide difference in the result."[68] I need scarcely wait to show the feebleness of this suggestion. When we remember the incalculable

---

[68] Darwin discussed this subject in Chapter 9 of the 6th edition of his book: DARWIN, Charles. *The origin of species*. 6th edition. London: John Murray, 1872. Darwin acknowledged that the sterility of first crosses and of hybrids could not have been acquired by natural selection (pp. 247-248) and was really unable to explain this phenomenon: "But why, in the case of distinct species, the sexual elements should so generally have become more or less modified, leading to their mutual infertility, we do not know; but it seems to stand in some close relation to species having been exposed for long periods of time to nearly uniform conditions of life." (p. 263). [RAM]

number of animal and vegetable species, living and extinct, we immediately feel the necessity for some much more general explanation of their existence than is furnished by supposing that their mutual sterility, which constitutes their most general or constant distinction, was in every case due to some incidental effect produced on the generative system by uniform conditions of life. To say nothing of the antecedent improbability, that in all these millions and millions of cases the reproductive system should happen to have been affected in this peculiar way by the merely negative condition of uniformity; there is, as it seems to me, the overwhelming consideration that, at the time when a variety is first forming, this condition of prolonged exposure to uniform conditions of life must necessarily be absent as regards that variety; yet this is just the time when we must suppose that the infertility with its parent form arose. For, if not, the incipient variety would at once have been re-absorbed into the parent form by intercrossing, as we shall see more fully under the next head of this criticism.

In view of these considerations I conclude that while Mr. Darwin has given the best of reasons to show why domesticated varieties have so rarely become sterile *inter se*, he has entirely failed to suggest any reason why this should so generally have been the case with natural species. [p. 343]

Swamping Effects of Intercrossing

On this subject Mr. Darwin writes, "Most animals and plants keep to their proper homes, and do not needlessly wander about; we see this with migratory birds, which almost always return to the same spot. Consequently, each newly-formed variety would generally be at first local, as seems to be the common rule with varieties in a state of nature; so that similarly modified individuals would soon exist in a small body together, and would often breed together. If the new variety were successful in its battle for life, it would slowly spread from a central district, competing with and conquering the unchanged individuals on the margin of an ever-increasing circle."*

Now, to my mind, these considerations do not dispose of the difficulty in question. In the first place, a very large assumption is made when the newly-formed variety is spoken of as represented by

---

* 'Origin of Species,' ed. 6, pp. 72-3 *et seq.*

"similarly modified individuals" – the assumption, namely, that the same variation occurs simultaneously in a number of individuals inhabiting the same area. Of course, if this assumption were granted, there would be an end of the present difficulty; for if a sufficient number of individuals were thus simultaneously and similarly modified, there need be no longer any danger of the variety becoming swamped by intercrossing. But the force of the difficulty consists in the very fact of this assumption being required to meet it. The theory of natural selection, as such, furnishes no warrant for supposing that the same beneficial variety should arise in a number of individuals simultaneously. On the contrary, the theory of natural selection trusts to the chapter of accidents in the matter of variation; and in this chapter we read of no reasons why the same beneficial variation should arise simultaneously in a sufficient number of individual cases to prevent its being swamped by intercrossing with the parent form. Or, to state the case in other words, in whatever measure the assumption in question is resorted to, in that measure is the theory of natural selection confessed inadequate to furnish an explanation of the origin of species. And to this must be added the important consideration already adduced, namely, that a very large proportion, if not the majority, of features which serve to distinguish species from species are features presenting no utilitarian significance; and [p. 344] therefore that, even if they were each conceded to have arisen in a number of individuals simultaneously, they would not have benefited those individuals in their struggle for existence with the parent form. Hence their re-absorption by intercrossing, would not be hindered by natural selection, which is the agency here invoked by Mr. Darwin to account for their continuance. This consideration, however, introduces us to the third and last of the difficulties with which the theory of natural selection is beset.

Inutility of Specific Characters

The only answer which Mr. Darwin makes to this difficulty is, that structures and instincts which appear to us useless may nevertheless be useful. But this seems to me a wholly inadequate answer. Although in many cases it may be true, as indeed it is shown to be by a number of selected illustrations furnished by Mr. Darwin, still it is impossible to believe that it is always, or even generally so. In other words, it is impossible to believe that in all, or even in most, cases where minute specific differences of structure or of instinct are to all appearance useless, they are nevertheless useful. Observe, the case would be different if the great majority of specific distinctions, like the great majority of larger distinctions, were of obvious utilitarian significance. In this case we might reasonably set down the exceptions as proof of the rule, or hold that they appear to be exceptions only on account of our ignorance. But it is certainly too large a demand upon our faith in natural selection to appeal to the argument from ignorance, when the facts require that this appeal should be made over so very large a number of instances. We might, for example, most reasonably conclude that the callosities on the hind legs of horses, or the instinct of covering their excrement shown by certain roaming Carnivora, are of some such hidden use to the animals as to have preserved them in their struggle for existence. I say, we might reasonably conclude this, provided that such instances were exceptional. But seeing that so enormous a number of specific peculiarities are in the same predicament, it surely becomes the reverse of reasonable so to pin our faith to natural selection as to conclude that all these peculiarities must be useful, whether or not we can perceive their utility. For by doing this we are but reasoning in a circle. The only evidence we have of natural selection is furnished by the observed utility [p. 345] of innumerable structures and instincts which for the most part are of generic, family, or higher order of taxonomic value. Therefore, unless we reason in a circle, it is not competent to argue that the apparently useless structures and instincts of specific value are due to some kind of utility which we are unable to perceive. But I need not argue this point, because in the later editions of his works Mr. Darwin freely acknowledges that a large proportion of specific distinctions must be conceded to be useless to the species presenting them; and, therefore, that they resemble the great and general distinction of mutual sterility in not admitting of any explanation by the theory of natural selection.[69]

Natural Selection not a Theory of the Origin of Species

---

[69] Romanes' account of those difficulties of the theory of evolution, and of Darwin's acknowledgement of being unable of explaining them by natural selection, is quite fair. [RAM]

In view of the foregoing considerations it appears to me obvious that the theory of natural selection has been misnamed; it is not, strictly speaking, a theory of the origin of *species*: it is a theory of the origin – or rather of the cumulative development – of *adaptations*, whether these be morphological, physiological, or psychological, and whether they occur in species only, or likewise in genera, families, orders, and classes[70]. These two things are very far from being the same; for, on the one hand, in an enormously preponderating number of instances, adaptive structures are common to numerous species; while, on the other hand, the features which serve to distinguish species from species are, as we have just seen, by no means invariably – or even generally – of any adaptive character. Of course, if this were not so, or if species always and only differed from one another in respect of features presenting some utility, then any theory of the origin of such adaptive features would also become a theory of the origin of the species which present them. As the case actually stands, however, not only are specific distinctions very often of no utilitarian meaning; but, as already pointed out, the most constant of all such distinctions is that of sterility, and this the theory of natural selection is confessedly unable to explain.

For these reasons I think there can be no doubt that the theory of natural selection ought to be recognized as exclusively a theory of the evolution of adaptive modifications; not therefore or necessarily a theory of the evolution of different species. And, if once this important distinction is clearly perceived, the [p. 346] theory in question is released from all the difficulties which we have been considering[71]. For these difficulties have beset the theory only because it has been made to pose as a theory of the origin of species; whereas, in point of fact, it is nothing of the kind. In so far as natural selection has had anything to do with the genesis of species, its operation has been, so to speak, incidental; it has only helped in the work of originating species in so far as some among the adaptive

---

[70] This point of Romanes' paper was regarded by the defenders of evolution theory as an unfortunate and dreadful piece of criticism of the very title of Darwin's book. Besides the rhetorical characteristics, Romanes' point is very serious: he claims that Darwin did not explain the origin of species – and that his own theory of physiological selection does explain it. [RAM]

[71] It is unlikely that Darwin would accept Romanes' suggestion that the theory of natural selection could only explain adaptive modification, since he did attempt to explain the origin of species and other problems of evolution theory. [RAM]

variations which it has preserved happen to have constituted differences of only specific value. But there is an innumerable multitude of other such differences with which natural selection can have had nothing to do – particularly the most general of all such differences, or that of mutual sterility – while, on the other hand, by far the larger number of adaptations which it has preserved are now the common property of numberless species.

Let it, therefore, be clearly understood that it is the office of natural selection to evolve adaptations – not therefore or necessarily to evolve species. Let it also be clearly understood that in thus seeking to place the theory of natural selection on its true logical footing, I am in no wise detracting from the importance of that theory[72]. On the contrary, I am but seeking to release it from the difficulties with which it has been hitherto illegitimately surrounded.*

Again, it is comparatively seldom that we encounter any difficulty in perceiving the utilitarian significance of generic and family distinctions, while we still more rarely encounter any such difficulty in the case of ordinal and class distinctions. Why, then, should we so often encounter this difficulty in the [p. 347] case of specific distinctions? Surely, because some cause other than natural selection must have been at work in the differentiation of species[73], which has

---

[72] Of course, Romanes' interpretation *does* lessen the importance of Darwin's theory. [RAM]

* It will be at once apparent how this release is effected. For, if it be clearly recognized that natural selection has to do with the evolution of species only in so far as specific distinctions happen to be of utilitarian character, all objections to the theory raised from its inability to explain the whole origin of species (or the general fact of sterility between allied species, and the frequently non-utilitarian character of specific distinctions) become irrelevant; whatever its professions may have been, in point of fact the theory has nothing to do with explaining any of these things, and, therefore, ought never to have been held responsible for their explanation. Again, as regards the difficulty from the overwhelming effects of intercrossing, this really concerns the theory of natural selection only in the case of varieties; not in that of species, genera, families, &c. Yet the work of natural selection in maintaining and perfecting adaptive structures in these higher taxonomic divisions is probably of quite as much importance as its work in seizing upon the earliest beneficial variations, although this fact has been lost sight of in the eagerness of naturalists to constitute the theory an explanation of the origin of species.

[73] The attitude of Darwin and of strict Darwinians was to use natural selection (and, sometimes, the inheritance of acquired characters) to explain all facts of evolution. Any difficulty found would be interpreted as a puzzle that would be solved in the

operated in a lesser degree in the differentiation of genera, and probably not at all in the differentiation of families, orders, and classes. Such a cause it is the object of the present paper to suggest; and if in the foregoing preamble it appears somewhat presumptuous to have insinuated that Mr. Darwin's great work on the 'Origin of Species' has been misnamed, I will conclude the preamble with a quotation from that work itself, which appears at once to justify the insinuation, and to concede all that I require[74].

"Thus, as I am inclined to believe, morphological differences, which we consider as important, such as the arrangement of the leaves, the division of the flower or of the ovarium, the position of the ovules, &c., first appeared in many cases as fluctuating variations, which sooner or later became constant through the nature of the organism and of the surrounding conditions, is well as through the intercrossing of distinct individuals; but not through natural selection; for as these morphological characters do not affect the welfare of the species, any slight variations in them could not have been governed or accumulated through this latter agency. It is a strange result which we thus arrive at, namely that characters of slight vital importance to the species are the most important to the systematist".* [p. 348]

---

future without any paradigmatic change. Romanes, however, proposes a paradigm amendment, introducing a new additional mechanism. [RAM]

[74] In the following citation, Darwin concedes that there are differences between species that cannot be explained by natural selection but are used in taxonomical practice. This does not imply (as Romanes suggests) that Darwin allowed that his theory could not explain the origin of species. [RAM]

* 'Origin of Species,' ed. 6, p.176. See also p. 365 *et seq*. The argument is that the guiding principle of classification being a hitherto unconscious tracing of the lines of genetic descent, and heredity not being more concerned with preserving useful variations than indifferent ancestral peculiarities, the latter are now of more use than the former to systematists, seeing that they have been allowed to persist without undergoing adaptive modification at the hands of natural selection. I have no doubt that this argument is sound; but the "strange result" to which it leads implies that natural selection has throughout been the cause of the origin of adaptations; not therefore necessarily, or even generally, of the origin of species. But let me not be misunderstood. In saying that the theory of natural selection is not, properly speaking, a theory of the origin of species, I do not mean to say that the theory has no part at all in explaining such origin. Any such statement would be in the last degree absurd. What I mean to say is that the theory is one which explains the origin or the conservation of adaptations, whether structural or instinctive, and whether these occur in species, genera, families, orders, or classes. In so far, therefore, as useful structures are likewise species-distinguishing structures, so far is the theory of their

Evolution of Species by Independent Variation

Enough has now been said to justify the view that there must be some cause or causes, other than natural selection, operating in the evolution of species. And this is no more than Mr. Darwin himself has expressly and repeatedly stated to have been his own view of the matter; nor am I aware that any of his followers have thought otherwise. Hitherto the only additional causes of any importance that have been assigned are use and disuse[75], sexual selection, correlated variability[76], and yet another principle which I believe to have been of much more importance than any of these – not even excepting the first, where the origin of species only is concerned. Yet it has attracted so little attention as scarcely ever to be noticed by writers on Evolution, and never even to have received a name. For the sake of convenience, therefore, I will call this principle the Prevention of Intercrossing with Parent Forms, or the Evolution of Species by Independent Variation.

First, let us consider how enormous must be the number of variations presented by every generation of every species. According to the Darwinian theory, it is only those variations which happen to have been useful that have been preserved; yet, even as thus limited, the principle of variability is held to have been sufficient to furnish material out of which to construct the whole adaptive morphology of nature. How immense, therefore, must be the number of unuseful variations. These are probably many hundred of times more numerous

---

origin also a theory of the origin of the species which present them. But useful structures and species-distinguishing structures are very far from being convertible terms. On the one hand, as we have seen, many useful structures are shared by many species in common; and, on the other hand, many species-distinguishing structures are not useful. Therefore I say that the theory which explains the origin of useful structures is not, strictly speaking, a theory of the origin of species; it only explains the origin of species in cases where it happens that one species differs from another in respect of features all of which present utilitarian significance. And this, as even Mr. Darwin himself allows, is very far from being universally, or even usually, the case.

[75] Darwin and most Darwinians accepted the inheritance of changes produced by use and disuse. [RAM]

[76] Romanes omitted other relevant factors discussed by contemporary authors, such as natural variability within species, geographical isolation, sudden changes (called "sports" by Darwin), a directive tendency towards evolution, etc. His strategy was focusing upon just a few points, showing their failures, and proposing his own theory as the "only" solution for those problems. [RAM]

than the useful variations, although they are all, as it were, stillborn, or allowed to die out immediately by intercrossing. Hence, as a matter of fact, we find that no one individual "is like another all in all;" which is another way of saying that a specific type may be regarded as [p. 349] the average mean of all individual variations, any considerable departure from this average being, however, checked by intercrossing.

But now, should intercrossing by any means be prevented, there is no reason why unuseful variations should not be perpetuated by heredity quite as well as useful ones when under the nursing influence of natural selection – as, indeed, we see to be the case in our domesticated productions. Consequently, if from any cause a section of a species is prevented from intercrossing with the rest of its species, we might expect that new varieties – for the most part of a trivial and unuseful kind – should arise within that section, and that in time these varieties should pass into new species. And this is just what we do find [77]. Oceanic islands, for example, are well known to be extraordinarily rich in peculiar species; and this can best be explained by considering that a complete separation of the fauna and flora on such an area permits them to develop independent histories of their own, without interference by intercrossing with their originally parent forms. We see the same principle exemplified by the influence of geographical barriers of any kind, and also by the consequences of migration. For when a species begins to disperse in different directions from its original home, those members of it which constitute the vanguard of each advancing army are much more likely to perpetuate any individual variations that may arise among them, than are the members which still occupy the original home. Not only is the population much less dense on the outskirts of the area occupied by the advance guard; but beyond these outskirts there lies a wholly unoccupied territory upon which the new variety may gain a footing during the progress of its further migration. Thus, instead of being met on all sides by the swamping effects of intercrossing with its parent form, the new variety is now free to perpetuate itself with

---

[77] Here, Romanes acknowledges the significance of geographical isolation for the rise of new species. This mechanism had been proposed by Moritz Wagner in 1868, but Darwin denied its importance. See MAYR, Ernst. Isolation as an evolutionary factor. *Proceedings of the American Philosophical Society*, **103**: 221-230, 1959. [RAM]

comparatively little risk of any such immediate extinction. And the result is that wherever we meet with a chain of nearly allied specific forms so distributed as to be suggestive of migration with continuous modification, the points of specific difference are trivial or non-utilitarian in character. Clearly this general fact is in itself enough to prove that, given an absence of overwhelming intercrossing, independent variability may be trusted to evolve new species. The evidence which I have collected, and [p. 350] am collecting, of this general fact must be left to constitute the subject of a future publication.*

Physiological Selection, or Segregation of the Fit

Were it not for the very general occurrence of some degree of sterility between allied species, and were it not also for the fact that closely allied species are not always, or even generally, separated from one another by geographical barriers†, one might reasonably be disposed to attribute all cases of species-formation by independent variability to the prevention of intercrossing by geographical barriers, and by migration. But it is evident that these two facts can no more be explained by the influence of geographical barriers, or by migration, than they can be by the influence of natural selection. It is therefore the object of the present paper to suggest an additional factor in the formation of specific types by independent variability, and one which appears to me fully competent to explain both the general facts just mentioned.

Of all parts of those variable beings which we call organisms, the most variable is the reproductive system. It is needless for me to remind any reader of Mr. Darwin's works what a mass of evidence be

---

* So far as I am aware, the first writer who insisted on the great importance of the prevention of intercrossing in the evolution of species, both by isolation and migration, was Moritz Wagner. Since then Wallace, Weismann, and others, as also Darwin himself, have in lesser degrees recognized this factor. The most recent contribution to the subject is by a Fellow of this Society, Mr. Charles Dixon, whose work on 'Evolution without Natural Selection' presents a large and admirable body of facts, showing the important part which the prevention of intercrossing has played in the evolution of species among Birds. But I cannot find that any previous writer has alluded to the principle which it is the object of the present paper to enunciate, and which is explained in the succeeding paragraphs.

† As Mr. Wallace observes, allied species usually occupy contiguous areas, which more often than not, are likewise continuous.

has accumulated, showing the extreme sensitiveness of the reproductive system to small changes in the conditions of life.

The consequent variations may occur either in the direction of increased fertility, as with our domesticated varieties, or in that of sterility in all degrees, as with wild species when confined. So extreme is the sensitiveness of the reproductive system in these respects – or, in other words, so liable is this system to vary – [p. 351] that in many cases, even when tamed in their own countries, allowed freedom, fed on their natural food, and so forth, animals become absolutely sterile. Moreover, so delicately is the reproductive system balanced in respect of variability, that sometimes it will change in the direction of sterility and sometimes in the opposite direction of increased fertility, under a change of conditions the same in kind, but different in degree. Lastly, in numberless individual cases variability occurs in either of these two opposite directions without any assignable reason at all, or, in Mr. Darwin's language, spontaneously. So that, on the whole, we must accept it as a fact that the reproductive system, both in plants and animals, is preeminently liable to vary, and this both in the direction of sterility and in that of increased fertility. Indeed, Mr. Darwin goes so far as to say: "It would appear that any change in the habits of life, whatever these habits may be, if great enough, tends to affect, in an inexplicable manner, the powers of reproduction." And he adds this important qualification: "The result depends more on the constitution of the species than on the nature of the change; for certain whole groups are affected more than others; but exceptions always occur, for some species in the most fertile groups refuse to breed, and some in the most sterile groups breed freely."

Now, having regard to all these delicate, complex, and for the most part hidden conditions which determine this double kind of variation within the limits of the reproductive system, there can be no difficulty in granting that variations in the direction of greater or less sterility must frequently occur in wild species. Probably, indeed, if we had any means of observing this point, we should find that there is no one variation more common; but of course, whenever it arises, whether as a result of changed conditions of life, or, as we say, spontaneously, it immediately becomes extinguished, seeing that the individuals which it affects are less able, if able at all, to propagate the variation; or, if the variation should extend to all the individuals of a species under a change of environment, that the species would become extinct.

Let these three points, then, be clearly kept in mind: 1st, that when a section of any species is cut off by geographical barriers, or by migration, from intercrossing with its parent form, it tends to run into new varieties, and so eventually to develop new [p. 352] species; 2nd, that the number of unuseful variations taking place in all species is incalculable; and 3rd, that the reproductive system is so especially variable, both intrinsically and in response to changed conditions of life, that increase of sterility[78] must often arise as a variation under nature.

I have now fully, if not tediously, prepared the way for explaining the suggestion which I have to make. From what has been said it may be concluded that all the multitude of individual variations perpetually occurring in every species become reabsorbed in the specific type by intercrossing, unless the variations happen to be either useful, to take place in isolation, or by way of what Mr. Spencer calls "direct equilibration," such as use, disuse, and so forth. It has also been shown that any variations in the reproductive system which take place in the direction of increased sterility must likewise tend to become extinguished. But now it must be added that there is one such variation in the reproductive system to which this remark does not apply. For if the variation be such that the reproductive system, while showing some degree of sterility with the parent form, continues to be fertile within the limits of the varietal form, in this case the variation would neither be swamped by intercrossing, nor would it die out on account of sterility. On the contrary, the variation would be perpetuated with more certainty than could a variation of any other kind. For, in virtue of increased sterility with the parent form, the variation would not be exposed to extinction by intercrossing; while, in virtue of continued fertility within the varietal form, the variation would perpetuate itself by heredity, just as in the case of variations generally when not re-absorbed by intercrossing. To make my meaning perfectly clear I will use an illustration.

Suppose the variation in the reproductive system is such that the season of flowering or of pairing becomes either advanced or retarded. Whether this variation be, as we say, spontaneous, or due to any change of food, habitat, climate, &c., does not signify. The only point we need here attend to is that some individuals, living on the

---

[78] An unpredictable increase *or decrease* of sterility, as Romanes has already conceded. [RAM]

same geographical area as the rest of their species, have varied in their reproductive systems, so that they can only propagate with each other[79]. They are thus perfectly fertile *inter se*, while absolutely sterile with all the other members of their species. This particular variation being communicated by inheritance to their progeny, there would soon arise on the same area, [p. 353] or, if we like, on closely contiguous areas, two varieties of the same species, each perfectly fertile within its own limits, while absolutely sterile with one another. That is to say, there has arisen between these two varieties a barrier to intercrossing which is quite as effectual as a thousand miles of ocean; the only difference is that the barrier, instead of being geographical, is physiological.

Now, from this illustration I hope it will be obvious that wherever any variation in the highly variable reproductive system occurs, tending to sterility with the parent form while not impairing fertility with the varietal form – no matter whether this is due, as here supposed, to a slight change in the season of reproductive activity, or to any other cause –there the physiological barrier in question must interpose, with the result of dividing the species into two parts. And it will be further evident that when such a division is effected, the same conditions are furnished to the origination of new species as are furnished to any part of a species when separated from the rest by geographical barriers. For now the two physiologically divided sections of the species are free to develop independent histories without mutual intercrossing.

Or, to state this suggestion in another way. If the suggestion is well founded, it enables us to regard a large proportion, if not the majority, of natural species as so many expressions of variation in the reproductive systems of their ancestors. When accidental variations of a non-useful kind occur in any of the other systems or parts of an organism, they are, as a rule, immediately extinguished by intercrossing. But whenever they happen to arise in the reproductive system in the way here suggested, they must inevitably tend to be preserved as new natural varieties or incipient species. Once formed as such, the new natural variety, even though living upon the same area as its parent species, will begin an independent course of history;

---

[79] One difficulty in Romanes' theory is the need to assume that *several individuals* have changed exactly in the same way, at the same time, becoming mutually fertile while being unable to reproduce with the unchanged individuals. [RAM]

and, as in the now analogous case of isolated varieties, will tend to increase its morphological distance from the parent form, until it eventually becomes a true species. At least it appears to me obvious that in so many cases as variations of the kind in question have taken place, in so many cases must the conditions have been supplied to the formation of new species. Later on I will show in more detail how these conditions have been utilized. [p. 354]

The principle thus briefly sketched in some respects resembles and in other respects differs from the principle of natural selection, or survival of the fittest. For the sake of convenience, therefore, and in order to preserve analogies with already existing terms, I will call this principle Physiological Selection, or Segregation of the Fit.

Arguments à priori

Before stating the evidence which I have been able to collect of the operation of this principle, it is desirable that I should make one or two general remarks upon the conditions under which alone this evidence can be presented.

First, let it be observed that if this particular kind of variation ever takes place at all, we are not concerned either with its causes or with its degrees. Not with its causes, because in this respect the theory of physiological selection is in just the same position as that of natural selection; it is enough for both that the needful variations are provided, without it being incumbent on either to explain the causes which underlie the variations. Nor is the theory of physiological selection concerned with the degrees of sterility which may in any particular cases have been initially supplied. For, whether the degree of sterility with the parent form is originally great or small, the result of it in the long run will be the same; the only difference will be that in the latter case a greater number of generations would be required in order to separate the varietal from the parent form, as a little thought will be enough to show.*

---

* Suppose that, on an average, a cross between the parent and the variety were to yield a progeny of 2, while a cross between two individuals of the new variety were to yield a progeny of 3. In this case there is but a very small degree of sterility towards the profit form; yet if figured out it will be found – supposing this degree, of sterility to be inherited by the pure-bred varieties – abundantly sufficient to ensure multiplication of the varietal type, without danger of this type being swamped by the parental.

Next, let it be observed that, from the nature of the case, we cannot expect to meet with much direct evidence of physiological selection yielded by our domesticated varieties. For, first, it has never been the object of breeders or horticulturists to go back to the wild stocks, and therefore observations on this point are wanting; second, breeders and horticulturists keep their strains separate, and many kinds of variation are preserved other than those [p. 355] of the reproductive system – with which alone we are concerned, and which must be extremely rare as compared with all the other kinds of variation that it is the aim of breeders and horticulturists to preserve; for, third, it is never the aim of these men to preserve this particular kind of variation. In view of these three considerations, it is clear that we cannot expect to derive much evidence of physiological selection from our domesticated varieties, further than the general proof which these afford of the primary importance of preventing intercrossing with parent forms, if a new varietal form is ever to gain a footing. No one of these domesticated varieties could have been what it now is, unless such intercrossing had been systematically prevented by man; and this gives us good reason to infer that no natural species could have been what it now is, unless every variety in which every species originated had been prevented from intercrossing with its parent form by nature. For we have seen that even if the initial variation, which, as a matter of fact, was in each case preserved, happened to have been useful – and this supposition is, as we have also seen, the reverse of true – it would still be so eminently liable to extinction by intercrossing, that it is at least doubtful whether its preservation could have been secured by natural selection alone. Hence, although we cannot obtain much direct evidence in favour of physiological selection from plants and animals under domestication, we do obtain from them such indirect evidence as arises from proof of the importance of preventing intercrossing with parent forms.

Again, as to plants and animals under nature, the particular variation with which alone we are concerned would probably not be noticed until it had given rise to a new species. In this respect, therefore, the theory of physiological selection is in the same predicament as that of natural selection; in neither case are we able directly to observe the formation of one species out of another by the agency supposed; and therefore in both cases our belief in the agency supposed must, to a large extent, depend on the probability established by general considerations. Nevertheless, although our sources of direct evidence are thus seen to be necessarily limited, I shall now hope to show that they are sufficient to prove the only fact which they are required to prove, namely, that the particular kind of variation which is in question does occur, both in nature and under domestication.

Although, as above remarked, the theory of physiological [p. 356] selection is not necessarily concerned with the causes of variation in the reproductive system, it will be convenient to classify these causes as extrinsic and intrinsic. By the extrinsic causes I mean changes in the environment which act upon the reproductive system, whether these be changes of food, climate, degree of liberty, and so forth. By intrinsic causes I mean changes taking place in the reproductive system itself of a kind depending on what Mr. Darwin calls "the nature of the organism," or on causes which we are not able to trace, and which may therefore be termed spontaneous.

Now the particular kind of variation the occurrence of which I have to prove is that of impotency – whether absolute or comparative – towards the parent form, without decrease of potency towards the varietal form. One very obvious example of this kind of variation has already been given in the season of flowering or of pairing being either advanced or retarded. This I conceive to be a most important case for us, inasmuch as it is one that must frequently arise in nature. Depending, as it chiefly does, on external causes, numberless species both of plants and animals must, I believe, have been segregated by its influence. For in every case where a change of food, temperature, humidity, altitude, or of any of the other many and complex conditions which go to constitute environment – whether the change be due to migration of the species, or to alterations going on in an area occupied by a stationary species – in every case where such a change either promotes or retards the season of propagation, there we have the kind of variation which is required for physiological selection. And it is needless to give detailed instances of its occurrence where this is due to so well-known and frequently-observed a cause.

But it is in what I have called the spontaneous variability of the reproductive system itself that I mainly rely for evidence of physiological selection. The causes of variability are here far more numerous, subtle, and complex than are, such extrinsic causes as those above mentioned; and they are always at work in the reproductive systems of all organisms. Moreover, sensitive as the reproductive system is to small changes in the conditions of life, its spontaneous variability is, as Mr. Darwin has shown, even more remarkable. Now, among all the possible variations of the reproductive system however caused, there is one which, whenever it is produced, cannot be allowed again to disappear; [p. 357] but must be perpetuated by the ever vigilant agency of physiological selection. What this particular variation is we now know, and I will proceed to give evidence of its spontaneous occurrence, first in individuals, second in varieties, and third in species.

1. *Individuals.* – Mr.Darwin observes: – "It is by no means rare to find certain males and females which will not breed together, though both are known to be perfectly fertile with other males and females. We have no reason to suppose that this is caused by these animals having been subject to any change in their habits of life; therefore such cases are hardly related to our present subject. The cause apparently lies in an innate sexual incompatibility of the pair when matched." He then proceeds to give examples from horses, cattle, pigs, dogs, and pigeons, concluding with the remark that "these facts are worth recording, as they show, like so many previous facts, on what slight constitutional differences the fertility of an animal often depends."[*] And in another place he gives references to similar facts in the case of plants.[†]

Now, if it were needful, I could supply a number of additional cases of this individual incompatibility, or of absolute sterility as between two individuals, each of which is perfectly fertile with all other individuals.[**] But I think that the not unusual occurrence of this fact will be regarded as abundantly substantiated by these references.

And here, it appears to me, we have a most significant piece of evidence upon the origin of species. If even as between two individuals there may thus arise absolute sterility, without there being in either of them the least impairment of fertility with other individuals, is it not obvious that we have precisely the kind of

---

[*] 'Variation,' &c., vol. ii. pp. 145-6.

[†] 'Origin of Species,' ed. 6, p. 246.

[**] I may remark that individual incompatibility is especially apt to declare itself when the individuals paired belong to different species. That is to say, while some individuals taken from the two species will readily produce hybrids, other individuals taken from the same species will prove hopelessly sterile. The same applies to the fertility of hybrids. These, facts are of some additional importance to us, because they occupy a kind of intermediate position between these given above and those, given in the next succeeding paragraphs.

variation which my theory requires, and that we have this variation spontaneously or suddenly given in the highest possible degree of efficiency? Shallow criticism might reply that this is the precise opposite of the variation which my theory requires; and under one point of view such is the case. For here we have [p. 358] sterility towards the varietal form, with unimpaired fertility towards the parent form. But a little thought will show that this criticism would be shallow. The important fact is that among a number of individuals of the same species, all exposed to apparently the same conditions of life, some of the number so far deviate from the specific type in respect of their reproductive systems as to be absolutely sterile with certain members of their own species, while remaining perfectly fertile with other members. In terms of the above criticism, therefore, this fact might be translated into saying that if the reproductive system can be proved to undergo so remarkable a variation as that of *individual* incompatibility, much more is it likely to undergo the "opposite" variation, wherein a similar incompatibility would extend to a larger number of individuals. For certainly the most remarkable feature about this individual incompatibility is the fact of its being only individual. It would not be nearly so remarkable, or physiologically improbable, that such incompatibility should run through a whole race or strain. Therefore, the fact of individual incompatibility appears to me to furnish most important evidence of my theory; for it proves that even the most apparently capricious and wholly unaccountable variations may spontaneously arise within the limits of the reproductive system – variations which, physiologically considered, are much more remarkable, or antecedently improbable, than anything that my theory requires.

2. *Races*. – But of even more importance to us is the direct evidence of such a state of matters in the case of varieties, breeds, or strains. Incompatibility between individuals is, indeed, of very great importance to my theory, because it constitutes the first link in a chain of direct evidence as to the actual occurrence of the particular kind of variation on which the theory depends; here we have, as it were, the first beginning in an individual organism of a change which, under suitable conditions, may give rise to a new strain, and so eventually to a new species. But, seeing that the individual is so small a constituent part of his species, unless his peculiar incompatibility has reference to the majority of other individuals, so that it becomes only the minority of the opposite sex with whom he can pair, the probability is that the

peculiar condition of his reproductive system would not be perpetuated by heredity, but would become extinguished by intercrossing. As I have already said, it is, physiologically considered, even more remarkable that such [p. 359] incompatibility should ever be exclusively individual than that it should be racial; and therefore, as likewise remarked, I regard these cases of individual incompatibility as of value to my theory chiefly because they prove the actual occurrence of the variation which the theory requires, and this as suddenly or spontaneously arising in the highest degree of efficiency. But I will now adduce evidence to show that a state of matters more or less similar may be proved to obtain throughout a whole breed or strain, so that we then have, not merely individual incompatibility, but what may be termed racial incompatibility; and therefore that we are on the highroad to the branching-place of a new species. Here I will again quote my facts from Darwin, partly because he has so profoundly studied the subject of variation, but chiefly because, wherever it is possible, I desire to rely upon his authority.

In the ninth chapter of the 'Origin of Species,' and in the nineteenth chapter of the 'Variation of Plants and Animals under Domestication,' Mr. Darwin adduces miscellaneous evidence of the fact that in many cases varieties of the same species exhibit a higher degree of fertility within themselves than they do with one another. In this respect, therefore, they resemble natural species. Inasmuch, however, as they are not natural species, but domesticated varieties (or the changed descendants of one natural species), they are here available as evidence to prove what I have just called racial incompatibility, due to the change which has been effected in their reproductive systems. It makes no difference whether we regard this change as due to intrinsic or to extrinsic causes; in either case the racial incompatibility is the same, and this is all that the theory of physiological selection requires. Take, for example, the following case which, as Mr. Darwin says, "is the result of an astonishing number of experiments made during many years on nine species of *Verbascum*, by so good an observer and so hostile[*] a witness as Gärtner: namely, that the yellow and white varieties when crossed produce less seed than the similarly coloured varieties of the same species;" and elsewhere he quotes a statement from the same

---

[*] "Hostile" because Gärtner believed that the distinction between species and varieties in respect of sterility is more absolute than Darwin believed.

authority to the effect that the blue and red varieties of the pimpernel are absolutely sterile together, while each is perfectly fertile within itself. So that in these cases we have a marked degree of racial incompatibility between [p. 360] yellow and white varieties, or between blue and red varieties of the same species, while each continues fertile within its own limits. And similarly in all the other cases.

Now, in these facts one may only see evidence of changes in the organism reacting on the reproductive system in such a way as to produce this particular effect. I shall have more to say on this subject later on; here it is enough to remark that it matters little to my theory whether the changes be thus due to reaction on the reproductive system, or have arisen in the reproductive system, as it were, independently; for, as above observed, whether the causes of the change be supposed intrinsic or extrinsic, the change itself is really all that we are now concerned with. This change, however produced, is a change in the direction of what I call racial incompatibility, and therefore, if it had taken place in any wild species, must necessarily have constituted a physiological barrier to intercrossing between the two varieties, which, according to my theory, is the primary condition required for the development of varieties into species. And that such a state of matters is at least as likely to occur in a wild species as in a domesticated descendant is obvious. For domestication, as a rule, increases fertility, and therefore is, as a rule, inimical to sterility, sometimes even breaking down the physiological barriers between natural species. Therefore, if at other times even under domestication the reproductive system may vary so as to erect these barriers between artificial varieties, much more are such barriers likely to be erected between varieties when these arise in a state of nature. Indeed, the difficulty is to find such cases in a state of domestication, the great difference between mongrels and hybrids consisting in this very fact of the former being so usually fertile, and the latter so usually sterile. But I trust that enough has now been said to show that even among our domestic productions we may find evidence of racial incompatibility, or of that particular variation in the reproductive apparatus which is required by the theory of physiological selection.

As regards varieties in a state of nature, it must be noticed, first of all, that racial incompatibility is not likely to be observed. For, on the one hand, if such incompatibility is in any degree pronounced, for this very reason the two forms would be ranked by naturalists as distinct species; while, on the other hand, if not so pronounced, the fact of incompatibility could only be revealed by careful observation. For these reasons the evidence which I [p. 361] have to give of incompatibility in a state of nature is derived chiefly from species, as I will now explain.

3. *Species.* – According to the general theory of evolution, which in this paper is taken for granted, the distinction between varieties and species is only a distinction of degree; and the distinction is mainly, as well as most generally, that of mutual sterility, whether absolute or partial. Therefore I am here supplied with an incalculable number of instances, all tending to support my theory; for in so many instances as variation has led to any degree of sterility between parent and varietal forms, or between the varying descendants of the same form, in so many instances it is a simple statement of fact to say that physiological selection must have taken place. There remains, however, the question whether the particular change in the reproductive system, which led to all these cases of mutual sterility, was anterior or posterior to changes in other parts of the organisms. For, if it was anterior, these other changes – even though they be adaptive changes – were presumably due to the sexual change having interposed its barrier to crossing with parent forms; while, if the sexual change were posterior to the others, the presumption would be that it was those other changes which, by their reaction on the reproductive system, induced the sexual change. I shall have to consider this alternative later on. Meanwhile, therefore, it is enough to point out that under either possibility the principles of physiological selection are present; only these principles are accredited with so much the more causal influence in the production of species in the proportion that we find reason to suppose the sexual change to have been, as a rule, the prior change. Hence, under either alternative, and on the datum that species are extreme varieties, we have presented many millions of instances of fertility within the varietal form, with sterility towards allied forms. Why, then, should we feel any difficulty in supposing that the same thing happens in a lesser degree? Nay, rather, would it not be a most extraordinary fact if it did never happen in lesser degrees? Yet, if it does ever happen in lesser degrees, we have a variation of the kind required by physiological selection, although not yet of a degree sufficient to constitute the variety a new species – seeing that species is practically a name reserved by naturalists to designate this particular kind of variation, when it has

arrived at a certain observable degree of departure from the parent form. [p. 362]

This way of looking at the matter may perhaps be rendered more effective if we glance for a moment at the extraordinary differences in the degrees of sterility which are manifested by variations that have gone far enough to be ranked by naturalists as undoubted species. For in this way we can see how impossible it is to lay down any hard and fast distinctions between species and varieties in respect of sterility, even though it has always been the aim of naturalists to give primary importance to this point. Now this difficulty is just what we ought to find, according to my theory, as a very few words will be enough to show. For, even if allied forms were always closely contiguous forms, we should expect on this theory that great differences in the degrees of sterility should be manifested by different species. According to this theory, species are but records of a sufficient degree of sterility having arisen with parent forms to admit of the varietal form not becoming swamped by intercrossing. Now, the degree of sterility required for this purpose would not be the same in all cases, seeing that in some cases other conditions might be present to assist in the prevention of intercrossing, as we shall see later on. Moreover, in other cases the initial (or the subsequently induced) degree of sterility may have been greater than was required to effect the physiological separation that took place. Lastly, when to these considerations we add that allied species are not always necessarily contiguous species, and therefore need never have had any opportunity of intercrossing (having originated independently from the same parent form in different localities) – when we consider all these things, we should expect to find the degrees of sexual incompatibility between species highly variable. Or, in other words, we should expect to find that the extreme varieties called species should not exhibit an equal degree of incompatibility in all cases. And this is just what we do find; or, as Mr. Darwin puts it, "the sterility of various species when crossed is so different in degree, and graduates away so insensibly, and, on the other hand, the fertility of pure species is so easily affected by various circumstances, that for all practical. purposes it is most difficult to say where perfect fertility ends and sterility begins."

But not only so. Among all the varieties in nature which are extreme enough to be ranked as species, we might expect, upon the theory of physiological selection, that some should have developed sterility towards certain of their allies, while developing [p. 363] an even increased degree of fertility towards others. For in all cases, according to this theory, degrees of fertility between allied forms are, so to speak, matters of accident; and it is only when variations in the direction of sterility with allied forms (parental or otherwise) are sufficiently pronounced to prevent intercrossing that the forms in question rise to specific rank. Therefore, looking to the immense number of species, we might expect that in some few cases where the allied forms are not also contiguous, the variation in the reproductive system which rendered one of the forms sterile with its parent form, should not also have rendered it sterile with exotic forms, or even that it should be more fertile with them than with itself. And this we do occasionally find to be the case, as the following quotations from Darwin will show.

"Of his [Herbert] many important statements I will here give only a single one as an example, namely, that "every ovule in a pod of *Crinum capense* fertilized by *C. revolutum* produced a plant, which I never saw to occur in a case of its natural fecundation." So that here we have perfect, or even more than commonly perfect, fertility in a first cross between two distinct species".[†]

Mr. Darwin then proceeds to give other and analogous cases as having been well observed in *Lobelia, Verbascum,* and *Passiflora*; and then adds, "In the genus *Hippeastrum,* in *Corydalis* as shown by Professor Hildebrand, in various orchids as shown by Mr. Scott and Fritz Muller, all the individuals are in this peculiar condition. So that with some species, certain abnormal individuals, and in other species all the individuals, can actually be hybridised much more readily than they can be fertilised by pollen from the same individual plant."

Now, these and all other such facts go to prove that, notwithstanding even a specific distinction, there may be a higher degree of compatibility between the sexual elements of the different forms than between the sexual elements of the same form; and this would show that in the matter of sexual compatibility more depends upon the nature of the sexual elements than depends upon the rest of the organism. In other words, we may here regard the two distinct species as (physiologically considered) extreme varieties, and thus we should have evidence of a higher degree of fertility between these two extreme varietal forms than [p. 364] normally occurs within each parent form. When, for instance, we are told by Gärtner that the

---

[†] Origin of Species,' ed. 6, p. 238; also see 'Variation,' vol. ii. pp. 143-4.

yellow and white varieties of one species of *Verbascum* are considerably more fertile with the similarly coloured varieties of distinct species than they are with the differently coloured varieties of the same species, we can only conclude that the state of the reproductive system is such that there is a higher degree of sterility – or a lesser degree of sexual affinity – within the limits of the parent form, than there is between it and another variety so far changed as to constitute a distinct species. I do not, of course, pretend that in these cases the species towards which the increased fertility is exhibited has been separated from the other by physiological selection. Indeed to do this would be to prove too much, because if the separation had been effected by physiological selection, there ought as a result to be increased sterility, and not increased fertility between these two particular specific forms. But I adduce these facts as forcible evidence of physiological selection, because they show, in the strongest imaginable way, that the conditions of sexual affinity which are required for physiological selection are to be found even between varieties so widely separated as to constitute true species. For if these conditions of sexual affinity may be such that an organism is actually more fertile with members of a distinct species than it is with members of its own species, much more may an organism which has become infertile with its parent form continue fertile with itself. In the cases mentioned the individual sexual organs may be regarded as relatively sterile towards their parent, i. e. their own specific form, while relatively fertile towards another specific form. Much more then may an individual be relatively sterile towards its parent form, while relatively fertile towards its own varietal form.

The same argument may be adduced from the case of animals. There are many recorded instances of both birds and mammals which, when under confinement, have proved themselves more fertile with members of different species than with members of their own. Now, whether this state of matters be supposed to be normal or superinduced by changes in the conditions of life, in either case we have organisms which are relatively sterile towards their own parent form, or relatively fertile towards another varietal form so different as to constitute a distinct species. As in the similar case of the plants above mentioned, therefore, we may here repeat how much more probable than [p. 365] this would be the case that is required by physiological relation – namely, a variety relatively sterile towards its parent form, while relatively fertile within itself.

These anomalous cases, however, have only been given to show the highly variable and capricious character of the reproductive system both in plants and animals; and hence to show that the much less remarkable kind of variation which is required by my theory is not antecedently improbable. But, as a matter of argument, I do not require these anomalous cases; for enough has been previously said to prove that the particular kind of variation required actually does occur as between individuals, between races, and between species. Nevertheless, for the sake of adducing yet one further argument of an *à priori* kind, I may notice the very general fact that different varietal characters in parents belonging to the same species persistently refuse to blend in the offspring. This, indeed, may be said to be the rule both in plants and animals.* But the varietal character with which we are concerned belongs to the reproductive system itself, independently of any other part of the organism. Therefore, if this variation follows the rule of variations in general, there must be more difficulty in its blending with the parent (or unchanged) form than there is in its blending with other similarly changed forms. But, in this particular case, failure to blend means failure to propagate – *i. e.* sterility, whether partial or absolute. The varietal form will thus be more fertile within itself than it is towards its parent stock.

Arguments à posteriori

Hitherto the evidence which I have adduced in favour of physiological selection as an agency in the evolution of species is only *prima facie*. That is to say, although we have evidence to show the occurrence of this particular kind of variation, and although we can see that whenever it does occur it must be preserved, as yet we have had no evidence to indicate to what extent this particular kind of variation has been at work in the formation of species. Thus far all I have been endeavouring to show is that we have many and weighty considerations of an *à priori* kind whereby to render the theory of physiological selection [p. 366] antecedently probable. I will, therefore, next proceed to state such evidence as I have been able to collect, tending to show that the facts of organic nature are such as we should expect they ought to be, if it is true that physiological selection

---

* See, for example, 'Variation of Plants and Animals under Domestication,' vol. ii. p. 72.

has played a considerable part in their causation. And to do this I will begin by taking the three cardinal objections to the theory of natural selection with which I set out, namely sterility, intercrossing, and inutility. For, as we shall see – and this in itself is a suggestive consideration – all the facts which here present formidable obstacles to the theory of natural selection are not only explained by the theory of physiological selection, but furnish to that theory some of the best evidence which I have been able to find.

Argument from Sterility between Species

As now repeatedly observed, the theory of natural selection is not, properly speaking, a theory of the origin of species: it is a theory of the development of adaptive structures. Only if species always differed from one another in respect of adaptive structures would natural selection be a theory of the origin of species. But, as we have already seen, species do not always, or even generally, thus differ from one another. In what, then, do they differ? They differ, first, chiefly and most generally, in respect of their reproductive systems; this, therefore, I will call the primary difference. Next, they differ in an endless variety of more or less minute details of structure, which are sometimes of an adaptive character, and sometimes not. These, therefore, I will call secondary differences. Now, these secondary differences, or differences of minute detail, are never numerous as between any two allied species; in almost all cases they admit of being represented by units. Yet, if it were possible to enumerate all the specific differences throughout both the vegetable and animal kingdoms, there would be required a row of figures expressive of many millions. Or, otherwise stated, the secondary features which serve to distinguish species from species are minute differences of structure, sometimes useful and sometimes not, which may occur in any parts of organisms, but which never occur in many parts of the same organism. Thus we perceive that, if we have regard to the whole range of species, what I call the secondary differences are in the highest imaginable degree variable or inconstant. The only distinction which is at all constant or general is the one which I call primary, or the one which belongs [p. 367] exclusively to the reproductive system. Surely, therefore, what we first of all require in a theory of the origin of *species* is an explanation of this relatively constant or general distinction. But this is just what all previous theories fail to supply. Natural selection accounts for some among the many secondary distinctions; but is confessedly unable to account for the primary distinction. The same remark applies to sexual selection, use and disuse, economy of growth, correlated variability, and so forth. Even the prevention of intercrossing by geographical barriers is unable to explain the very general occurrence of some degree of sterility between two allied varieties, which have diverged sufficiently to take rank as different species. All these theories, therefore, are here in the same predicament: they profess to be theories of the origin of species, and yet none of them is able to explain the one fact which more than any other goes to constitute the distinction between species and species. The consequence is that most evolutionists fall back upon a great assumption: they say it must be the change of organization which causes the sterility; it must be the secondary distinctions which determine the primary. But the contrary proposition is surely at least as probable, namely, that it is the sterility which, by preventing intercrossing with parent forms, has determined the secondary distinctions; or, rather, that this has been the original condition to the operation of the modifying causes in all cases where free intercrossing has not been otherwise prevented. For, obviously, it is a pure assumption to say that the secondary differences between species have been historically prior to the primary difference, and that they stand to it in the relation of cause to effect. Moreover, the assumption does not stand the test of examination, as I will now proceed to show.

First, on merely *à priori* grounds, it scarcely seems probable that whenever any* part of any organism is slightly changed in any way by natural selection or any other cause, the reproductive system should forthwith respond to that change by becoming sterile with allied forms. What we find in nature is a more or less constant association between the one primary distinction and an endless profusion of secondary distinctions. Now, if this association had been between the primary distinction and some one, or even some few, secondary distinctions, constantly the [p. 368] same in kind, in this case I could seen that the question would have been an open one as to which was cause and which effect, or which was the conditional and which the conditioned. But, as the case actually stands, on merely antecedent

---

* This appears to be what the theory requires, seeing that *all* parts of organisms are subject to secondary specific distinctions.

grounds it does not appear to me that the question is an open one. Here we have a constant peculiarity or condition of the reproductive system, repeated over and over again millions of times, throughout organic nature past and present; and we perpetually find that when this peculiar condition of the reproductive system occurs it is associated with structural changes elsewhere, which, however, may affect any part of any organism, and this in any degree. Now, I ask, is it a reasonable view to imagine that the one constant peculiarity is always the result and never the condition of any among these millions of inconstant and organically minute changes with which it is found associated? Even if I had no theory whereby to account for the primary and constant distinction being also the primordial and conditioning distinction, on merely *à priori* grounds I should feel convinced that in some way or another it *must* be so.

But, secondly, quitting *à priori* grounds, it is a matter of notorious fact that in the case of nearly all our innumerable artificial productions, organisms admit of being profoundly changed in a great variety of ways, without any reaction on the reproductive system following as a consequence. So seldom, indeed, does any such reaction follow from what may be termed all these innumerable experiments upon the subject, that Mr. Darwin was obliged to explain the discrepancy between the known influence of artificial selection and the supposed influence of natural selection by invoking a wholly independent, an extremely hypothetical, and, to my mind, a most unsatisfactory principle. This principle – *i. e.* that of prolonged exposure to similar conditions of life – I have already considered, and shown why it appears to me the feeblest suggestion that is to be met with in the whole range of Mr. Darwin's writings.

Thirdly, as regards wild species, Mr. Darwin shows that "the correspondence between systematic affinity and the facility of crossing is by no means strict. A multitude of cases could be given of very closely allied species which will not unite, or only with extreme difficulty; and, on the other hand, of very distinct species which unite with the utmost facility." And he goes on to show that "within the limits of the same family, or even of [p. 369] the same genus, these opposite cases may occur".* Now, on the supposition that sterility

---

* He also adds: – "No one has been able to point out what kind or amount of difference in any recognizable character is sufficient to prevent two species crossings. It can be shown that plants most widely different in habit and general

between species is always or generally caused by the indirect influence on the reproductive system of changes taking place in other parts of the organism, these facts are unintelligible – being, indeed, as a mere matter of logic, contradictory of the supposition.

Fourthly, it is surely a most significant fact that, as Mr. Darwin observes, "independently of the question of fertility, in all other respects there is the closest general resemblance between hybrids and mongrels"[†]. For this fact implies that natural selection and artificial selection run perfectly parallel in all other respects, save in the one respect of reacting on the reproductive system, where, according to the views against which I am arguing, they must be regarded as differing, not only constantly, but also profoundly.

Fifthly, and lastly, Darwin further observes that "the primary cause of the sterility of crossed species (as compared with crossed varieties) is confined to differences in their sexual elements" [‡]. Now this assuredly proves that the primary specific distinction is one with which the organism as a whole is not concerned; this primary distinction is, so to speak, a local variation in the organism, which has to do only with the reproductive system, and which therefore need not necessarily be in all, or even in most, cases an incidental result of minute variations going on elsewhere.

In view of these several considerations, it appears to me perfectly plain that the smaller organic changes which alone are concerned in specific distinctions are not always, or even generally, adequate to react on the reproductive system [p. 370] in the way hitherto supposed by evolutionists[*]; but that the primary distinction is in most cases, as I have just expressed it, a local variation in the organism, which has to

---

appearance, and having strongly marked differences in every part of the flower, even in the pollen, in the fruit, and in the cotyledons, can be crossed. Annual and perennial plants, deciduous and evergreen trees, plants inhabiting different stations and fitted for extremely different climates, can often be crossed with ease. And, after considering the further case of reciprocal crosses, he expresses the general conclusion: "Such cases are highly important, for they prove that the capacity in any two species to cross is often completely independent of their systematic affinity, that is of any difference in their structure or constitution, excepting in their reproductive systems." ('Origin of Species,' ed. 6, p. 243).

[†] 'Origin of Species,' where the general fact is proved beyond question.

[‡] *Loc. cit.* This fact, also, is proved beyond the possibility of question.

[*] I do not think that Mr. Darwin himself entertained this supposition, and therefore I have not his authority against me.

do only with the reproductive system. Why, then, should we suppose that it differs from a local variation taking place in any other part of the organism? Why should we suppose that, unlike all other such variations, it cannot be independent, but must be superinduced as a secondary result of variations taking place elsewhere? It appears to me that the chief reason why evolutionists suppose this, is because the particular variation in question happens to have as its result the origination of species; and that, being already committed to a belief in other agencies as the cause of such origination, in consistency they are obliged to regard this particular kind of local variation as not independent, but superinduced as a secondary result of these other agencies operating on other parts of the organism. In short, it appears to me that by persistently regarding the primary specific distinction as a derivative and incidental result of the secondary, evolutionists are putting the cart before the horse; and the only reason they can show for choosing this arrangement is that they already assume the origin of species to have been due to other causes, and in particular to natural selection. But once let them clearly perceive that natural selection is concerned with the origin of species only in so far as it is concerned with the origin of adaptive structures, or only in so far as it is concerned with some among the many secondary distinctions – once let naturalists be perfectly clear upon this point, and they will perceive that the primary specific distinction takes its place beside all other variations as a variation of a local character, which may, indeed, at times be due to the indirect influence of natural selection, use, disuse, and so forth; but which may also be due to any of the other numberless and hidden causes that are concerned with variation in general.

Thus, I repeat, what we require in a theory of the origin of species is a theory to explain the primary and most constant distinction between species, or the distinction in virtue of which they exist as species. This distinction, as we have now so repeatedly seen, is one that belongs exclusively to the reproductive system; and it always consists in comparative sterility towards [p. 371] allied forms, with continued fertility within the varietal form. Now, this state of matters as between allied species is merely an intensification, or a further development, of that which physiological selection supposes to obtain between the physiological varieties, where the variation is from the first in the direction just mentioned. That this initial variation should afterwards become intensified by the practical separation of the two varieties, so that what began as a varietal difference ends as a specific difference, is no more than we should expect. For from the first the variation was one specially affecting the reproductive system in the special way required; intercrossing with the parent form was from the first precluded in a degree proportional to the amount of the variation. The species was thus from the first divided into two physiological parts, each of which then entered upon an independent course of genetic history; the principle of continued variation alone the same lines would tend to increase the original separation; the new variety, therefore, besides having been thus started with a tendency, and a probable increasing tendency, to a physiological separation from its parent stock, must afterwards have become exposed to all or any such modifying causes as are found to produce a similar separation in a portion of a species when started on an independent course of history by migration or by geographical isolation.

Lastly, over and above all these considerations, there remains one of much importance, not only to the present division of my argument, but to my theory as a whole. For Mr. Darwin has furnished exceedingly good reasons for entertaining his own view that this is "one of the causes of ordinary variability; namely, that the reproductive system, from being eminently sensitive to changed conditions of life, fails under these circumstances to perform its proper function of producing offspring closely similar in all respects to the parent form"[+]. Now, if this view is well founded – and, as I have said, Mr. Darwin's arguments in favour of it are most cogent – it obviously has most important bearings on the present theory; for it implies that whenever the reproductive system undergoes a variation on its own account, whether this be due to extrinsic or intrinsic causes, it is apt to induce variations in other parts of progeny. Hence, prevention of intercrossing by the physiological barrier of reproductive or primary variation is so far more likely to be followed [p. 372] by secondary variations than when the prevention of intercrossing arises from geographical barriers or from migration. For in this case, over and above the influence of independent variability, there is a direct causal connection between the agency which prevents intercrossing and the subsequent production of secondary specific characters. So that, if Mr. Darwin's view of one of the causes of variability be accepted, it follows that wherever the primary specific

---

[+] 'Origin of Species,' ed. 6, p. 260.

distinction of sterility arises, there it is to be expected that an unusual crop of variations should follow by way of consequence in other parts of the physiologically separated progeny – variations, therefore, which, whether they happen to be useful or unuseful, appear under circumstances most favourable to their perpetuation as secondary specific characters.

I trust, then, that sufficient reasons have now been given to justify my view that, if we take a broad survey of all the facts bearing on the question, it becomes almost impossible to doubt that the primary specific distinction is, as a general rule, the primordial distinction. I say "as a general rule," because the next point which I wish to present is that it constitutes no part of my argument to deny that in some, and possibly in many, cases the primary distinction may have been superinduced by the secondary distinctions. Indeed, looking to the occasional appearance of partial sterility between domesticated productions, as well as to the universally high degree of it between genera, and its universally absolute degree between families, orders, and classes, I see the best of reasons to conclude that in some cases the sterility between species may have been originally caused, *and in a much greater number of cases subsequently intensified*, by changes going on in other parts of the organism. Moreover, I doubt not that, of the agencies determining such changes, natural selection is probably one of the most important. In other words, I do not doubt that natural selection, by operating independently on a separated portion of a species – whether the separation be physiological or geographical – may often help to induce sterility with the parent form, by indirectly modifying the reproductive system through changes which it effects in other parts of the organism; and I see no reason to doubt that the same is true of sexual selection, use and disuse, economy of growth, correlated variability, or any other cause tending to modify the organism in any of its parts, and so, in *some* instances, reacting indirectly on the reproductive system in the way required. Here I only [p. 373] differ from other evolutionists in refusing to suppose that this must invariably, or even generally, be the result of what I may term adaptational causes, when these are producing small (i. e. specific) morphological changes in any part of any organism. Yet, as I have said, I doubt not that such has been the incidental or indirect result of these causes in some minority of cases. But, now, what does this amount to? It amounts to nothing more than a re-statement of the theory of physiological selection. It merely suggests hypothetically the cause, or causes, of that particular variation in the reproductive system with which alone the theory of physiological selection is concerned, and which, as a matter of fact, *however caused*, is found to constitute the one cardinal distinction between species and species. Therefore I am really not concerned with what I deem the impossible task of showing how far, or how often, natural selection, or any other cause, may have induced this particular kind of variation in the reproductive system by its operations on other parts of an organism. Even if I were to go the full length that other evolutionists have gone, and regard this primary specific distinction as in all cases due to the secondary specific distinctions, still I should not be vacating my theory of physiological selection; I should merely be limiting the possibilities of variation within the reproductive system in what I now consider a wholly unjustifiable manner. For, as previously stated, it appears to me much the more rational view that the primary specific distinction is likewise, as a rule, the primordial distinction, and that the cases where it has been superinduced by the secondary distinctions are comparatively few in number.

Next, let it be observed that, even in these last-mentioned cases – whether, as I believe, they are comparatively few or comparatively numerous – where the primary distinction has been superinduced by the secondary, even in these cases my theory is available to show why the two kinds of distinction are so generally associated, or why it is that the primary distinction is so habitual an accompaniment of the secondary distinctions, of whatever kinds or degrees the latter may happen to be. For, according to my theory, the reason of the association in these cases is that it can only be those kinds and degrees of secondary distinction which are able so to react on the reproductive system as to induce the primary distinction that are *for this reason* preserved, or allowed to become developed as a new specific type. Whether as causes or as effects, therefore, the secondary distinctions are *dependent* [p. 374] on the primary one, in the sense that, even if they be the causes, they depend for their existence on the fact that they happen to have been capable of producing this particular effect – a general view of the case which appears to me abundantly justified by the fact of their general *association*. Hence, if there are any cases – and I do not doubt that there are many – where the secondary distinctions have been the cause of the primary distinction, still even here the former are, as I have phrased it, dependent on the latter, inasmuch as the latter is a necessary condition to their existence. Or, otherwise expressed, unless the secondary distinctions had happened to be of a kind which induced the primary distinction, they could not in themselves have survived, but would have been reabsorbed by free intercrossing. Thus, according to my view, even in the minority of cases where the causes of the primary distinction have been such changes in the organism as I have called secondary distinctions, even in this minority of cases the principles of physiological selection have been at work. For these principles have in all those cases *selected* the particular kinds of secondary distinctions which have proved themselves capable of so reacting on the reproductive system as to bring about the primary distinction.

Suppose, for instance, that all our horticulturists and breeders were suddenly to allow all domesticated varieties freely to intercross, and suppose that some of these varieties had been previously acted upon by artificial selection to an extent of inducing sterility in a degree comparable with what evolutionists imagine that natural selection may have been able to accomplish in incipient species. Under these circumstances, physiological selection would at once set to work to pick out all these sexually protected forms, and hand them on as permanent varieties (or, if the sterility were sufficiently pronounced, as true species); while all the other forms, no matter how much they might differ from one another in respect of secondary distinctions, would be doomed to extinction – or, as we should then say, to reversion, which merely means reabsorption of secondary distinctions into parent forms. Now, if so soon as the artificial barriers to intercrossing were removed this is what would inevitably take place, even with secondary distinctions already formed, is it not evident that, in the original absence of any kind of barrier otherwise given, none of these secondary distinctions could ever have arisen, except those [p. 375] which happened so to react on the reproductive system as themselves incidentally to erect a barrier, which might then serve – as in the parallel case given in my illustration – to protect that particular assemblage of secondary distinctions from extermination when they first arose, and afterwards to admit of their being handed on in ever-increasing degrees of development? And, in point of fact, that this has been the case (supposing for illustration's sake the primary to have always been the result of secondary distinctions) is proved by the very general association that is now found to subsist between them – an association which can only be accounted for by supposing that all other kinds of secondary distinction failed in what may be termed their struggle for existence, simply because they were not able to rear for themselves this barrier of sterility.

Thus, we see, it really makes no essential difference to my theory whether it be, supposed, in any given case, that the primary distinction was prior or subsequent to the secondary distinctions. I have given my reasons for believing that in the great majority of cases the primary distinction was, as I have said, the primordial distinction; and, if so, the causal influence of physiological selection in the formation of species was in these cases absolute. But I have also given my reasons for believing that in a minority of cases the secondary distinctions determined the primary distinction; and, if so, the causal influence of physiological selection was in these cases relative, or conditional on other causes extrinsic to the organism. But whether the ultimate causes of the primary distinction be extrinsic or intrinsic, and whether this primary distinction be historically prior or subsequent to the secondary distinctions, in all cases (save where intercrossing is otherwise presented) it must be physiological selection that has been the agency to which the preservation of the secondary distinctions has been due. For, as we have now so repeatedly seen, any secondary distinctions, however useful in themselves, must be always liable to extraction almost at the moment of their birth, unless they happen to be protected by the primary distinction. Hence, whether the latter be given by independent variation on the part of the reproductive system itself, or as an indirect and concomitant result of variations taking place elsewhere, it is equally true that the principles of physiological selection have been at work; and, therefore, that it is to those [p. 376] principles we must look for our ultimate explanation of the origin of species*.

If we thus regard sterility between species as the result of what I have called a local variation arising only in the reproductive system, whether induced by changes taking place in other parts of the organism, to changes in the conditions of life, or to changes inherent in the reproductive system itself, we can understand (*a*) why such sterility rarely, though sometimes, occurs in our domesticated

---

* In order to avoid needlessly confusing the foregoing argument, I have omitted to notice that geographical barriers serve the same function as physiological barriers; and also that secondary distinctions caused by use and disuse do not require to be protected from the levelling effects of intercrossing. But, as will be seen from the next succeeding paragraphs, these considerations are in no way opposed to my theory.

productions; (*b*) why it so generally occurs in some degree between species; and (*c*) why as between species it occurs in all degrees.

(*a*) It rarely occurs in our domesticated productions, because it has never been the object of breeders or horticulturists to preserve this kind of variation. Yet it sometimes does occur in some degree among our domesticated productions, because the changes produced on other parts of the organism by artificial selection do, in a small percentage of cases, react upon the reproductive system in the way of tending to produce sterility with the parent form, without lessening fertility with the varietal form. Again (*b*), this particular condition of the reproductive system is so generally characteristic of species, simply because, as a general rule, it is owing to this condition that species exist as species; any variation, therefore, towards this condition, howsoever produced, must always have been preserved by physiological selection, with the result of a new specific form to record the fact. And, lastly (*c*), this particular variation in the reproductive system has taken place under nature in such a number of degrees, from absolute sterility between species up to complete, or even to more than complete fertility, because natural species, while being records of this particular *kind* of variation, are likewise the records of all *degrees* of such variation which have proved sufficient to prevent overwhelming intercrossing with parent forms. Sometimes this degree has been less than others, because other conditions – climatic, geographical, habitational, physiological, and even psychological – have co-operated to prevent intercrossing, or even to render [p. 377] the prevention of intercrossing wholly unnecessary, and thus not in any way to require the protecting influence of physiological selection. I will consider these points separately.

First, other conditions may co-operate with physiological selection to prevent intercrossing with parent forms, and therefore, in whatever degree such co-operation is furnished, a correspondingly less degree of sterility will be required in order to secure a differentiation of specific type. Of these other conditions, migrations and geographical barriers are probably the most important; and as such barriers may occur in all degrees of efficiency, from wholly secluding small sections of species in oceanic islands, to imposing but slight difficulties in crossing streams, &c., it is evident that in many cases physiological selection may be thus assisted in a great variety of degrees. Again, even where there are no geographical barriers of any kind, varieties will occasionally be segregated by their different degrees of adaptation to differences of climate – the adaptation having no special reference to the reproductive system, and yet, by determining that the variety shall live under a different climate from the parent form, more or less effectually preventing intercrossing with that form. The same thing applies to varieties occupying stations of their own[†], and also, in the case of higher Vertebrata, to all the members of the same variety preferring to pair together, rather than with their parent form, or with other varieties[‡]. In all these cases where the principles of physiological selection have been in any degree accidentally assisted by other conditions, a correspondingly less degree of variation in the reproductive system would have been needed to differentiate the species. That is to say, if the variation has been sufficient in amount, or in relation to all the other conditions of the time, to prevent intercrossing with the parent form in any extinguishing degree, the resulting sterility need not always be absolute, even as between compatriots, but may occur in any corresponding degree; while, as between species which have been independently evolved on different geographical areas, fertility may remain unimpaired, or even be accidentally increased.

Secondly, in other cases species may have become differentiated without the variations requiring to be protected from intercrossing, either by physiological, geographical, or any other barriers. In these cases, therefore, physiological selection has had no part in [p. 378] the evolution of species. The cases to which I allude are those where specific types have been modified by the agencies of what Mr. Spencer calls "direct equilibration ." Of these agencies the most important that happen to be known to us are use and disuse. A little thought will show that the moulding power of these agencies on specific types must be quite as independent of physiological selection as it is of natural selection. But a little more thought will show that this moulding influence must always be in some one line of morphological change: it cannot proceed in many diverging ways at once; but must slowly transmute a whole specific type into some other specific type. Now, if this change should happen to go on in a portion of a species living in one part of the world, when that portion becomes transmuted into different specific type, there is no reason why the now modified descendants should prove barren when crossed with their

---

[†] See 'Origin of Species,' ed. 6, p. 8.
[‡] *Ibid.*

unchanged, or differently changed, parent-form, which may be still living in any other part of the world.

In view of all these considerations, I should regard it as a serious objection to my theory if it could be shown that sterility between allied species is invariably absolute, or even if it could be shown that there are no cases of fertility unimpaired. What my theory would expect to find is exactly what we do find, namely, a considerable majority of instances where sterility occurs in all degrees, with comparatively exceptional instances where secondary distinctions have been able to develop without being associated with the primary distinction.

On the whole, therefore, I cannot but candidly consider that all the facts relating to the sterility of natural species are just what they ought to be, if they have been in chief part due to the principle which I am advocating. Mr. Darwin appears to have clearly perceived that there must be some one principle serving to explain all these facts, so curiously related and yet so curiously diverse; for he says, and he says most truly, "We have conclusive evidence that the sterility of species must be due to some principle quite independent of natural selection." And I trust enough has now been said to show that, in all probability, this hitherto unnoticed principle is the principle of physiological selection.

Argument from the Prevention of Intercrossing

This argument is the same from whatever cause the prevention of intercrossing may arise. Where intercrossing is prevented by [p. 379] geographical barriers or by migration, it is more easy to prove the evolution of new species as a consequence than it is when intercrossing has been prevented by physiological barriers; for in the latter case the older and the newer forms will probably continue to occupy the same area, and thus there will be no independent evidence to show that the severance between them was due to the prevention of intercrossing. Nevertheless, all the evidence which I have, of the large part that geographical barriers and migration have played in the evolution of species by the prevention of intercrossing with parent forms, goes to show the probable importance of physiological barriers when acting in the same way. Hence it will be better to postpone this line of argument till the appearance of my next paper, where I shall hope to show, from evidence furnished by the geographical distribution of species, how predominant a part the prevention of intercrossing has played in the evolution of species. Here, therefore, it will be enough to offer a few general remarks.

In the first place, the theory of physiological selection has this great advantage over the theory of natural selection, namely, that the swamping effects of free intercrossing on the new variety – or on the incipient species – are supposed to be from the first excluded by the very fact of the variation itself. This is so obvious an advantage that it appears needless to dwell upon its consideration.

But, in the next place, I may observe that, in so many cases as species do originate by physiological selection, the subsequent influence of natural selection admits of being considerably enhanced. For when once this physiological separation between a variety and its parent stock has been effected, there will be less likelihood than before of any useful variations which may subsequently arise in the former being again obliterated by intercrossing. This is evident, because the possibilities of intercrossing would now be restricted to a much smaller number of individuals, and therefore the influence of intercrossing would not be so detrimental to the continuance of any beneficial variation. In other words, the primary variation of the reproductive system would serve to protect any secondary variations of a useful kind which might afterwards arise elsewhere; just as happens in the analogous ease where intercrossing is prevented by geographical barriers, or by migration in different directions of varying descendants from a common centre. [p. 380]

And here we catch sight of another respect in which physiological selection probably cooperates with natural selection. As previously remarked, Mr. Darwin felt profoundly the strength of this objection from sterility between species, and, I may now add, he tried to imagine some way in which the general fact of such sterility might be reasonably attributed to natural selection. If he could have done this, of course, he would have mitigated the difficulty; for, as be writes, "it would clearly be advantageous to two varieties or incipient species if they could be kept from blending, on the same principle that, when man is selecting at the same time two varieties, it is necessary that he should keep them separate." But, as the result of his discussion, he concludes: "In considering the probability of natural selection having come into action in rendering species mutually sterile, the greatest difficulty will be found to be in the existence of many graduated steps from slightly lessened fertility to absolute sterility. It may be admitted that it would profit an incipient species, even if it were rendered in some slight degree sterile when crossed with its parent-form or with some other variety; for thus fewer bastardized and deteriorated offspring would be produced to commingle their blood with the new species in process of formation. But he who will take the trouble to reflect on the steps by which this first degree of sterility could be increased through natural selection to that high degree which is common with so many species, will find the subject extraordinarily complex. After mature reflection it appears to me that this could not have been effected through natural selection."

Now, with this conclusion I fully agree; but it will by this time be clearly seen that what cannot be effected by natural selection may well be effected by physiological selection. For both the considerations which Mr. Darwin here candidly adduces as insuperable difficulties in the way of supposing sterility due to natural selection, are just the considerations which most strongly favour the hypothesis of physiological selection. These two considerations are, first, "the many graduated steps from slightly lessened fertility to absolute sterility," and, second, "the steps by which this first degree of sterility would be increased." Now, as already shown in a previous part of this paper, these "many graduated steps" are just what we might expect to find on the theory of physiological selection; while, upon this theory, there is no need to suppose that "the first degree of sterility" must necessarily go on increasing. In [p. 381] whatever degree the sterility first occurs, in that degree it may remain; for, *ex hypothesi*, it must from the first have been sufficient to cause at least so much of physiological separation of the varietal type as to admit of the continuance of that type. If this degree of sterility were from the first but small, a longer time would be required to effect a complete separation between the parent and the variety, than if this degree were from the first considerable. But, as we have before seen, this is all the difference that would arise; and therefore, upon my theory, we may regard degrees of sterility as matters of no significance – although I do think it is extremely probable that when once sterility in any degree has arisen it will afterwards become increased, not so much for the reason assigned by Mr. Darwin (viz. prolonged exposure to uniform conditions), as from the general tendency which variations of all kinds present to continue in the lines of their initial deviation. I cannot doubt that if the theory of physiological selection had occurred to Mr. Darwin, he would have seen in this latter consideration a much more cogent reason than the one which he assigns for the general sterility that obtains between species. But he was precluded from applying this consideration because it did not occur to him that sterility might itself be originally due to independent variation, and thus itself be subject to the laws of variation in general.

I trust, then, that these considerations will have shown that, although natural selection cannot have, been directly instrumental in causing sterility between an incipient species and its parent form, if the incipient species were such in virtue of a variation in its reproductive system tending from the first to prevent intercrossing with its parent form, then there would be a variation the further development of which might be favoured by natural selection. For if, as Mr. Darwin thought, "it would profit an incipient species if it were rendered in some degree sterile with its parent form," although this profit could not have been initially conferred by natural selection, yet when it once arises from a spontaneous variation in the reproductive system itself, I see no reason to doubt that it should forthwith be favoured by natural selection, just as is the case with favourable variations in general. That is to say, natural selection would set a premium upon infertility with the parent form, and would thus cooperate with physiological selection in splitting up the specific type. For, although natural selection is powerless to induce sterility between allied forms, [p. 382] when once this sterility is given as an independent variation, the forms – though not necessarily the *individuals* – which profit by it would be favoured by natural selection in their competition with other forms which do not present such variation. In short, once let intercrossing with the parent-type be prevented by physiological selection, and the field is at once thrown open to the further or cooperating influence of natural selection – whether this be effected directly, as here supposed, or indirectly by modifying the reproductive system through the rest of the organism, as previously supposed. Later on, under Divergence of Character, I will show another and much more important respect in which physiological selection, by preventing intercrossing with parent forms, is able to assist natural selection in the differentiation of specific types.

Argument from the Inutility of Specific Differences

With reference to inutility, after what has already been said, I will only repeat this somewhat important question, – Why is it that apparently useless structures and instincts occur in such profusion among species, in much less profusion among genera, and scarcely at all among families, orders, and classes? To this question the Darwinist can only answer that the utility of apparently useless structures really is less than that of structures whose utility is observable. For although the argument from ignorance may be available up to a certain point, it clearly cannot be available to the extent of showing why useful structures within the limits of species should have their utility more disguised than useful structures elsewhere. Hence the Darwinist can only conclude that, at all events the majority of structures which he assumes to be useful in the case of species are not seen by him to be useful, because their utility actually is less than in the case of structures distinctive of genera, families, and so forth. He must argue that the points wherein species differ from species – being points of smaller detail than those which serve to distinguish genera, families, &c. – present less opportunity of usefulness; and, therefore, as a rule, actually are of too little use to admit of their utility being diagnosed, although not of so little use as to have prevented their development by natural selection, which is a better diagnostitian [sic] of utility than the naturalist. But how much more probable is the answer which [p. 383] may be furnished by any one who accepts the theory of physiological selection. For, upon this theory, it is quite intelligible that when a varietal form is differentiated from its parent form by the bar of sterility, any little meaningless peculiarities of structure or of instinct should at first be allowed to arise, and that they should then be allowed to perpetuate themselves by heredity, until, – not being conserved by natural selection – they should be again eliminated as so surplusage in the struggle for existence, whether by the economy of growth or by independent variation when undirected by natural selection. A greater or less time would in different cases be required to effect this reduction; and thus we can understand how it is that any useless structures which do not impose much tax upon the organism occasionally persist even into genera, but rarely into families, or higher taxonomic divisions.

This appears to me much the most probable view, not merely on *à priori* grounds, but also for the following reasons. I have just said that if apparently useless structures (whether these be new structures or modifications of old ones, slight changes of form, colour, and so forth) are thus to be regarded as really useless, or as meaningless variations not yet eliminated by natural selection or other agencies, – I have said that, if this is so, these apparently useless structures must be of a kind which do not impose much tax upon the organism. Now I have applied this test, and I find it is almost an invariable rule (both in plants and animals) that apparently useless structures are structures of this kind. Either on account of their small size or of their organically inexpensive material, they are structures which do not impose any such physiological tax upon the organism as should lead us to expect their speedy removal. But surely there can be no imaginable association between utility as disguised and smallness of size, or inexpensiveness of material. Whereas, no less surely, there is a most obvious connection between these things and real inutility. Thus, it is only a blind prepossession in favour of survival of the fittest as in all cases the originating cause of species that can lead to so irrational an assumption as that of universal utility.

Again, even apart from all the above considerations, the truth of this remark may be well exemplified within the limits of Mr. Darwin's own writings; for Mr. Darwin is here, as usual, his own best critic. He says, "In the earlier editions of this work I [p. 384] underrated, as it now seems probable, the frequency and importance of modifications due to spontaneous variability"*, by which he means unuseful modifications. And he proceeds to give a number of examples.

Elsewhere (p. 158) he points out that modifications which appear to present obvious utility are found on further examination to be really useless. This latter consideration, therefore, may be said to act as a foil to the one against which I am arguing, viz. that modifications which appear to be useless may nevertheless be useful. But here is a still more suggestive consideration, also derived from Mr. Darwin's writings. Among our domesticated productions, changes of structure – or even structures wholly new – not unfrequently arise which are in every way analogous to the apparently useless distinctions between wild species. Take, for example, the following most instructive case: –

"Another curious anomaly is offered by the appendages described by M. Eudes-Deslongechamps as often characterizing the Normandy

---

* 'Origin of Species,' ed. 6, p. 171. Also, and even more strongly, 'Descent of Man,' p. 367.

pigs. These appendages are always attached to the same spot, to the corners of the jaws; they are cylindrical, about three inches in length, covered with bristles, and with a pencil of bristles rising out of a sinus on one side; they have a cartilaginous centre with two small longitudinal muscles; they occur either symmetrically on both sides of the face, or on one side alone. Richardson figures them on the gaunt old 'Irish Greyhound pig;' and Nathusius states that they often occasionally appear in all the long-eared races, but are not strictly inherited, for they occur or fail in the animals of the same litter. As no wild pigs are known to have analogous appendages, we have at present no reason to suppose that their appearance is due to reversion; and if this be so, we are forced to admit that a somewhat complex, though apparently useless, structure may be suddenly developed without the aid of selection"[*].

Now, if any such structure as this occurred in a wild species, and if anyone were to ask what is the use of it, those who rely on the argument from ignorance would have a much stronger case than they usually have; for they might point to the cartilage supplied with muscles, and supporting a curious arrangement [p. 385] of bristles as much too specialized a structure to be wholly meaningless. Yet we happen to know that this particular structure is wholly meaningless. What, then, are we to say to the argument from ignorance in other and less cogent cases? I think we must say that the argument is wholly untrustworthy in fact, while even in theory it can only stand upon the assumption (latterly discarded even by Darwin himself) that all specific differences must be due to natural selection.

Argument from Divergence of Character

Any theory of the origin of species in the way of descent must be prepared with an answer to the question, Why have species *multiplied*? How is it that, in the course of evolution, species have not simply become transmuted in linear series instead of ramifying into branches? This question Mr. Darwin seeks to answer "from the simple circumstance that the more diversified the descendants from any one species become in structure, constitution, and habits, by so much will they be better enabled to seize on many and widely diversified places in the ecology of nature, and so be enabled to

---

[*] 'Variation,' &c. vol. i. pp. 78-9.

increase in numbers."* And he proceeds to illustrate this principle by means of a diagram, showing the hypothetical divergence of character undergone by the descendants of seven species. Thus, he attributes divergence of character exclusively to the influence of natural selection.

Now, this argument appears to me unassailable in all save one particular; but this is a most important particular: the argument wholly ignores the fact of intercrossing with parent forms. Granting to the argument that intercrossing with parent forms is prohibited, and nothing can be more satisfactory. The argument, however, sets out with showing that it is in limited areas, or in areas already overstocked with the specific form in question, that the advantages to be derived from diversification will be most pronounced. Or, in Mr. Darwin's words, it is where they "jostle each other most closely" that natural selection will set a premium upon any members of the species which may depart from the common type. Now, in as much as this jostling or overcrowding of individuals is a needful condition to the agency of natural selection in the way of diversifying character, must we not feel that the general difficulty from intercrossing previously [p. 386] considered is here presented in a special and aggravated form? At all events, I know that, after having duly and impartially considered the matter, to me it does appear that unless the swamping effects of intercrossing with the parent form on an overcrowded area is in some way prevented to begin with, natural selection could never have any material supplied by which to go on with. Let it be observed that I regard Mr. Darwin's argument as perfectly sound where it treats of the divergence of *species*, and of their further divergence into *genera*; for in these cases the physiological barrier is known to be already present. But in applying the argument to explain the divergence of *individuals* into *varieties*, it seems to me that here, more than anywhere else, Mr. Darwin has strangely lost sight of the formidable difficulty in question; for in this particular case so formidable does the difficulty seem to me, that I cannot believe that natural selection alone could produce any divergence of specific character, so long as all the individuals on an overcrowded area occupy that area together. Yet, if any of them quit that area, and so escape from the unifying influence

---

* 'Origin of Species,' ed. 6, p. 87.

of free intercrossing†, these individuals also escape from the conditions which Mr. Darwin names as those that are needed by natural selection in order to produce divergence. Therefore, it appears to me that, under the circumstances supposed, natural selection alone could not produce divergence; the most it could do would be to change the whole specific type in some one direction (the needful variations in that one direction being caused by some general change of food, climate, habit, &c., affecting a number of individuals simultaneously), and thus induce transmutation of species in a linear series, each succeeding member of which might supplant its parent form. But in order to secure diversity, multiplication, or ramification of species, it appears to me obvious that the primary condition required is that of preventing intercrossing with parent forms at the origin of each branch, whether the prevention be from the first absolute, or only partial. And, after all that has been previously said, it is needless again to show that the principles of physiological selection are at once the only principles which are here likely to be efficient, and the principles which are fully capable of doing all that is required. For species, as they now [p. 387] stand, unquestionably prove the fact of ramification; and it appears to me no less unquestionable that ramification, as often as it has occurred, can only have been permitted to occur by the absence of intercrossing with parent forms. But, apart from geographical barriers (which, according to Mr. Darwin's argument, would be inimical to the divergence of character by natural selection), the ramification can only take place as a consequence of physiological selection, or as a consequence of some change in the reproductive system which prevents intercrossing with unchanged (or differently changed) compatriots. But when once this condition is supplied by physiological selection, I have no doubt that divergence of character may then be promoted by natural selection, in the way that is explained by Mr. Darwin.

And this latter consideration is a most important one for us to bear in mind, because it furnishes an additional reason for the fact that when a section of a species has become physiologically separated from the rest of its species, it forthwith begins to run into variations of other kinds, and so eventually to differ from the parent type, not only

---

† As Mr. Darwin elsewhere observes, "Intercrossing plays a very important part in nature by keeping the individuals of the same species, or of the same variety, true and uniform in character" (p. 81).

as regards the primary distinction of sterility, but also as regards secondary distinctions which may affect any part of the organism. The only reasons which I have hitherto assigned for this fact are, first, that from the time when overwhelming intercrossing with the parent form is prevented, the varietal form is allowed to develop an independent course of varietal history, as in the parallel case where intercrossing is prevented by geographical barriers, or by migration; and, second, that when the primary variation takes place in the reproductive system, it is apt to cause secondary variations in the progeny. But now I may make this important addition to those reasons – the addition, I mean, that when intercrossing with a parent form is in any degree prevented by physiological selection, the varietal form is free to develop diversity of character under the influence of natural selection, in the way that has been so ably shown by Mr. Darwin.

From which it will be seen that the theory of physiological selection has this advantage over the theory of natural selection in the way of explaining what Mr. Darwin calls diversification of character, or what I have called the ramification of species. This diversification or ramification has reference chiefly to the secondary specific distinctions which, as we have seen, the theory of natural selection supposes to be the first changes that occur, and [p. 388] by their occurrence to induce the primary distinction of sterility. My theory, on the other hand, inverts this order, and supposes the primary distinction to be likewise, as a rule, the primordial distinction.

Now, the advantages thus gained are two-fold. In the first place, as just shown, we are able to release the principles of natural selection from what appears to me the otherwise hopeless difficulty of effecting diversification of specific character on an overcrowded area, with nothing to prevent free intercrossing; and, in the next place, as we can now see, we are able to find an additional reason for the diversification of character, over and above the one that is relied upon by Mr. Darwin. For, by regarding the primary distinction of sterility as likewise the primordial distinction, we are able to apply to an incipient variety, inhabiting even an overcrowded area, the same principles which are known to lead to diversification on oceanic islands, &c., as previously explained. Moreover, from any initial variation on the part of the reproductive system, we should be prepared to expect variations to occur in other parts of the progeny. Thus, if once we regard the primary distinction of sterility as also the initial distinction, instead of an incidental result of secondary distinctions, Mr. Darwin's argument touching the causes of diversification is not merely saved: it is notably extended by the addition of two independent principles which, as we know from other evidence, are principles of high importance in this respect.

Argument from Geographical Distribution

From the nature of the case, there is only one other line of evidence open whereby to substantiate the theory of physiological selection, namely, the evidence which is afforded by the geographical distribution of species. But the evidence here is both abundant in quantity and, to my mind, most cogent in quality. On the present occasion, however, I can only give a brief sketch of its main outlines.

Mr. Darwin has adduced very good evidence to show that large areas, notwithstanding the disadvantages which (on his theory) must arise from free intercrossing, are what he terms better manufactories of species than smaller areas, such as oceanic islands. On the other hand, I have previously noticed that oceanic islands are comparatively rich in peculiar species. But these two statements are not incompatible. Smaller areas are, as a rule, rich in peculiar species relatively to the number of [p. 389] their inhabitants; but it does not follow that they are rich in species if contrasted with larger areas containing very many more inhabitants. Therefore, the rules are that large areas turn out an absolutely greater number of specific types than small areas; although, relatively to the number of individuals or amount of population, the small areas turn out a larger number of species than the large areas.

Now, these two complementary rules admit of being explained as Darwin explains them. Small and isolated areas are rich in species relatively to the amount of population, because, as we have before seen, this population has been permitted to develop an independent history of its own, shielded from intercrossing with parent, and from struggle with exotic forms. On the other hand, large and continuous areas are favourable to the production of numerous species, first, because they contain a large population, so favouring the occurrence of numerous variations; and, secondly, because the large area furnishes a diversity of conditions in its different parts, as to food, climate, altitude, and so forth.

Such being the state of the facts, it is obvious that physiological selection must have what may be termed a first-rate opportunity of assisting in the manufacture of species on large areas. For, not only is it upon large and continuous areas that the antagonistic effects of intercrossing are most pronounced (and, therefore, that the influence of physiological selection must be most useful in the work of species-making); but here also the large population, as well as the diversity in the external conditions of life which the large area supplies to different parts of that population, – both these circumstances cannot fail to furnish physiological selection with a greater abundance of that particular variation in the reproductive system on which its action depends. For all these reasons, therefore, we might have expected, upon my theory, that large and continuous areas should be good manufactories of species.

Again, Mr. Darwin has shown that not only large areas, but likewise "dominant" genera upon those areas, are rich in species. By dominant genera he means genera represented by numerous individuals, as compared with other genera inhabiting the same area. This general rule he explains by the consideration that the qualities which first led to the form being dominant must have been useful qualities; that these would be transmitted to the otherwise varying offspring; and, therefore, that when these [p. 390] offspring had varied sufficiently to become new species, they would still enjoy their ancestral advantages in the struggle for existence. And this, I doubt not, is in part a true explanation; but I also think that the reason why dominant genera are rich in species is chiefly because they everywhere present a great number of individuals exposed to relatively great differences in their conditions of life, or, in other words, that they furnish the best raw material for the manufacture of species by physiological selection, as explained in the last paragraph. For, if the fact of dominant genera being rich in species is to be explained only by natural selection, it appears to me that the useful qualities which have already led to the dominance of the ancestral type ought rather to have proved inimical to its splitting up into a number of subordinate types. If already so far "in harmony with its environment" as to have become for this reason dominant, one would suppose that there is all the more reason for its not undergoing change by the process of natural selection. Or, at least, I do not see why the fact of its being in an unusual degree of harmony with its environment should in itself constitute any unusual reason for its modification by survival of the fittest. On the other band, as just observed, I do very plainly see why such a reason is furnished for the modifying influence of physiological selection.

Let us next turn to another of Mr. Darwin's general rules with reference to distribution. He took a great deal of trouble to collect evidence on the two following facts, namely: Ist, that "species of the larger genera in each country vary more frequently than the species of the smaller genera"; and 2nd, that "many of the species included within the larger genera resemble varieties in being very closely, but unequally, related to each other, and in having restricted ranges."*. By larger genera he means genera containing many species; and he accounts for these general facts by the principle "that where many species of a genus have been formed, on an average many are still forming." But how forming? If we say by natural selection alone, we should expect to find the multitudinous species differing from one another in respect of features presenting utilitarian significance; yet this is precisely what we do not find. For Mr. Darwin's argument here consists in showing that "in large genera the amount of difference between the species is often exceedingly [p. 391] small, so that in this respect the species of the larger genera resemble varieties more than do the species of the smaller genera." Therefore the argument, while undoubtedly a very forcible one in favour of the fact of *evolution*, appears to me scarcely consistent with the theory of *natural selection*. On the other hand, the argument tells strongly (though unconsciously) in favour of physiological selection. For the larger a genus, or the greater the number of species it contains, the greater must be the opportunity afforded for the occurrence of that particular kind of variation on which the principle of physiological selection depends. All the species of a genus may be regarded as so many varieties which have already been separated from one another physiologically; therefore each of them may now constitute a new starting-point for a further and similar separation – particularly as, in virtue of their previous segregation, many of them are now exposed to different conditions of life. Thus, it seems to me, we can well understand why it is that genera already rich in species tend to grow still richer; while such is not the case in so great a degree with genera that are poor in species. Moreover, we can well understand that, multiplication of species being in the first instance determined by changes in the reproductive system alone, wherever a large number of new species

---

* 'Origin of Species,' ed. 6, pp. 44, 45.

are being turned out, the secondary differences between them should be "often exceedingly small" – a general correlation which, so far as I can see, we are not able to understand on the theory of natural selection.

The two subsidiary facts, that very closely allied species have restricted ranges, and that dominant species are rich in varieties, both seem to tell more in favour of physiological than of natural selection. For "very closely allied species" is but another name for species which scarcely differ from one another at all except in their reproductive systems; and, therefore, the more restricted their ranges, the more certainly would they have become fused by intercrossing with one another, had it not been for the barrier of sterility imposed by the primary distinction. Or rather, I should say, had it not been for the original occurrence of this barrier, these now closely-allied species would never have become species. Again, that dominant species should be rich in varieties is what might have been expected; for the greater the number of individuals in a species, the greater is the chance of variations taking place in all parts of the organic type, and particularly in the [p. 392] reproductive system, seeing that this system is the most sensitive to small changes in the conditions of life, and that the greater the number of individuals composing a specific type, the more certainty there is of some of them encountering such changes. Now, of all the variations going on in all parts of the organic type, those which occur in the reproductive system of the kind required by physiological selection are most likely to be preserved, seeing that all other variations are likely to be swamped by free intercrossing. Hence, the richness of dominant species in varieties is, I believe, mainly due to the greater opportunity which such species afford of some degree of sterility arising between its constituent members.

Here is another general fact, also first noticed by Darwin, and one which be experiences some difficulty in explaining on the theory of natural selection. He says: – "In travelling from north to south over a continent, we generally meet at successive intervals with closely-allied or representative species, evidently filling the same place in the economy of the land. These representative species often meet and interlock, and as one becomes rarer and rarer, the other becomes more and more frequent, till the one replaces the other. But if we compare these species where they intermingle, they are generally as absolutely distinct from each other in every detail of structure as are specimens taken from the metropolis of each ... . In the intermediate region, having intermediate conditions of life, why do we not now find closely-linking intermediate varieties? This difficulty for a long time quite confounded me. But I think it can in large part be explained"‡.

This explanation is that, as "the neutral territory between two representative species is generally narrow in comparison with the territory proper to each, ... and as varieties do not essentially differ from species, the same rule will probably apply to both; and, therefore, if we take a varying species inhabiting a very large area, we shall have to adapt two varieties to two large areas, and a third variety to a narrow intermediate zone." It is hence argued that this third or intermediate variety, on account of its existing in lesser numbers, will probably be soon overrun and exterminated by the larger populations on either side of it. But surely this argument overlooks one all-important fact, namely, that varieties *do* "essentially differ from species" in [p. 393] respect of being able freely to intercross with one another. Therefore, how is it possible "to adapt two varieties to two large areas, and a third (transitional) variety to a narrow intermediate zone," in the face of free intercrossing on a continuous area? Let A, B, and C represent the three areas in question.

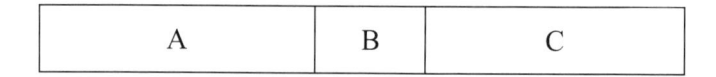

A	B	C

According to the argument, variety A passes first into variety B, and then into variety C, while variety B eventually becomes exterminated by the inroads both from A and C. But how can all this have taken place with nothing to prevent intercrossing throughout the entire area A B C? I confess that to me it seems this argument can only hold on the supposition that the analogy between varieties and species extends to the reproductive system; or, in a sense more absolute than the argument has in view, that "varieties do not essentially differ from the species" which they afterwards form, but from the first showed some degree of sterility towards one another. And, if so, we have of course to do with the principles of physiological selection.

That in all such cases of species-distribution these principles have played an important part in the species-formation, appears to be

---

‡ 'Origin of Species,' ed. 6, pp. 134-135.

rendered further probable from the suddenness of transition on the area occupied by contiguous species, as well as from the completeness of it – i. e. the absence of connecting forms. For all these facts combine to testify that the transition was originally due to that particular change in the reproductive systems of the forms concerned, which still enables those forms to "interlock" without intercrossing.

But this leads us to another general fact, also mentioned by Darwin, and well recognized by all naturalists, namely, that closely allied species, or species differing from one another in trivial details, usually occupy contiguous areas; or, conversely stated, that contiguity of geographical position is favourable to the appearance of species closely allied to one another. Of course this fact speaks in favour of evolution; but where the question is as to method, I confess that the theory of natural selection appears to me wholly irrelevant. For in all the numberless cases to which I allude, the points of minute detail wherein the allied species differ in respect of secondary distinctions are points [p. 394] which present no utilitarian significance. And, as previously argued, it is impossible to believe that there can be any general or constant correlation between disguised utility and insignificance of secondary distinction.

Now, the large body of facts to which I here allude, but will not at present wait to specify, appear to me to constitute perhaps the strongest of all my arguments in favour of physiological selection. Take, for instance, a large continental area and follow across it a chain of species, each link of which differs from those on either side of it by the most minute and trivial distinctions of a secondary kind, but all the links of which differ from one another in respect of their reproductive systems, so that no one member of the series is perfectly fertile with any other member. Can it be supposed that in every case this constant primary distinction has been superinduced by the trivial secondary distinctions, distributed as they are over different parts of all these kindred organisms, and yet nowhere presenting any but the most trifling amount of morphological change? Or, even if we were to suppose this, we have still to meet the question, How were all these trifling changes produced in the face of free intercrossing on the continuous area? Certainly not by natural selection, seeing that they are useless to the species presenting them. Let it then be by changes in the conditions of life, whether of food, of climate, or of any thing else. I can conceive of no other alternative. Yet if we accept this alternative, we are but espousing –in a disguised and roundabout way to be sure – the theory of physiological selection. For we are thus but hypothetically assigning the causes which have induced the primary distinction in each case, or the causes which have led to the mutual sterility. For my own part, I believe that the assignation would be, in the great majority of such cases, incorrect. That is to say, for reasons already given, I do not believe that in the great majority of such cases the trivial secondary distinctions, howsoever these were caused, can have had any thing to do with the great primary distinction. What I believe is, that all the closely allied species inhabiting our supposed continent, and differing from one another in so many points of minute detail, are but so many records of one particular kind of variation having taken place in the reproductive systems of their ancestors, and so often as it did take place, having necessarily given birth to a new species. The primary distinction [p. 395] thus became the constant distinction, simply because it was in virtue of this distinction, or in virtue of the variation which first originated this distinction, that the species became species; and the secondary distinctions thus became multitudinous, minute, and unmeaning, simply because they were of later origin, – the result of spontaneous variability, unchecked by intercrossing with the parent forms, and, on account of their trivial (*i.e.* physiologically harmless) nature, unchecked also by natural selection, economy of growth, or any other principle which might have prevented spontaneous variability of any other kind.

Relations between Survival of the Fittest and Segregation of the Fit

In several preceding parts of this paper, I have had occasion to notice some of the relations between the two forms of selection, natural and physiological. But it seems desirable to consider this matter a little more closely.

First of all, it will have been observed that the theory of physiological selection in some respects resembles and in other respects differs from that of natural section. Thus to some extent the two theories resemble one another in the kind of evidence by which they are each supported. In neither case does the theory rest upon any actual observation of the origin of species by the agency supposed; in both cases, therefore, the evidence of the agency is deduced from general considerations regarding the morphology and distribution of specific forms, as well as the observable relations in which such forms now stand to one another. Thus, in the case of each theory alike, the argument takes the form of first establishing a prima facie case, showing the antecedent probability of the cause in question; and next in proving, by a general survey of organic nature, that many of the facts are such as they ought to be if the theory in question is true.

So far, then, the two theories are logically similar in form; but in certain material points they widely differ.

To begin with, it is obvious that as natural selection is a theory of the origin of adaptations, it is a theory of the origin of genera, families, orders, and classes, quite as much as it is a theory of the origin of species. Indeed, as I have already given reasons to show, it appears to me that natural selection is much more a [p. 396] theory of the origin of genera, families, orders, and classes, than it is a theory of the origin of species. Physiological selection, on the other hand, is almost exclusively a theory of the origin of species, seeing that it can but very rarely have had anything to do with the formation of genera, and can never have had anything at all to do with the formation of families, orders, or classes. Hence, the evidence which we have of the evolutionary influence of physiological selection, unlike that which we have of the evolutionary influence of natural selection, is confined within the limits of specific distinctions.

Again, physiological selection differs from natural selection in that the variations on the occurrence of which it depends are variations of an unuseful kind. But, if the principle acts at all, it must resemble natural selection in being quite as vigilant in the selection, and quite as potent in the formation of organic types; seeing that any variation in the reproductive system of the kind in question must be preserved by the principle in question, and this with even more certainty than are the useful variations which furnish material to the working of natural selection. For while these useful variations – especially in their incipient stages, when few in number and unpronounced in character – are obviously exposed to the most serious risk of extinction from intercrossing, there is no such risk in the case of this non-useful variation. Here the obliterating effects of intercrossing on the now variety are from the first excluded by the very fact of its being a variety, or in virtue of the very peculiarity which distinguishes it as a variety.

Physiological selection therefore, has this great advantage over natural selection, – although it is confined to selecting only one kind of variation, and this only in the reproductive system, whenever this one kind of variation occurs it cannot escape the preserving agency of physiological selection. Hence, even if it be granted that the variation which affects the reproductive system in this particular way is a variation of comparatively rare occurrence, still, as it must always be preserved whenever it does occur, its influence in the manufacture of specific types must be cumulative, and, therefore, in the course of geological time, probably immense.

So much, then, for the resemblances and the differences between the two theories. It only remains to add that the two are complementary . I have already shown some of the respects in which the newer theory comes to the assistance of the older, and this in [p. 397] the places where the older has stood most in need of assistance. In particular, I have shown that segregation of the fit entirely relieves survival of the fittest from the difficulty under which it has hitherto laboured of explaining why it is that sterility is so constantly found between species, while so rarely found between varieties which differ from one another even more than many species; why so many features of specific distinction are useless to the species presenting them; and why it is that incipient varieties are not obliterated by intercrossing with parent forms. Again, we have seen that physiological selection, by preventing such intercrossing, enables natural selection to promote diversity of character, and thus to evolve species in ramifying branches instead of in linear series – a work which I cannot see how natural selection could possibly perform unless thus aided by physiological selection. Moreover, we have seen that although natural selection alone could not induce sterility between allied types, yet when this sterility is given by physiological selection, the forms which present it would be favoured in the struggle for existence; and thus again the two principles are found playing, as it were, into each other's hands . And here, as elsewhere, I believe that the co-operation enables the two principles to effect very much more in the way of species-making than either of them could effect if working separately. On the one hand, without the assistance of physiological selection, natural selection would, I believe, be all but overcome by the adverse influences of free intercrossing – influences all the more potent under the very conditions which are required for the multiplication of species by divergence of character. On the other hand, without natural selection, physiological selection would be powerless to create any differences of specific type, other than those of mutual sterility and trivial details of structure, form, and colour – differences wholly without meaning from a utilitarian point of view. But in their combination these two principles appear to me able to accomplish what neither can accomplish alone – namely, a full and satisfactory explanation of the origin of species.

General Summary and Conclusion

Seeing that the theory of natural selection is confessedly unable to explain the primary specific distinction of sterility, as well as a large proportional number of the secondary specific distinctions; seeing also that, even as regards the remainder, it is [p. 398] difficult to see how natural selection alone could have evolved them in the presence of free intercrossing; seeing all this, it becomes obvious that natural selection is not a theory of the origin of species[80]: it is a theory of the genesis of adaptive modifications, whether these happen to be distinctive of species only, or likewise of higher taxonomic divisions. Only, if species were always distinguishable in points of utilitarian significance, if natural selection were able fully to explain the fact of their mutual sterility, and if it were a part of the theory to show that in some way the mutual crossing of varieties is prevented; only under these circumstances could it be properly said that a theory of the genesis of adaptive modifications is likewise a theory of the origin of species. But, as matters stand, supplementary theories are required. Of these, the only ones hitherto suggested are the theories of use and disuse, sexual selection, correlated variability, prolonged exposure to similar conditions of life, and prevention of intercrossing by geographical barriers, or by migration[81]. The first three may here be neglected, as they do not touch the subject-matter of the present paper. Prolonged exposure to similar conditions of life has been shown inadequate to explain the contrast between hybrids and mongrels in respect of fertility. The prevention of intercrossing by geographical barriers and by migration has been shown adequate to account for the frequent appearance of non-adaptive specific characters. But the great distinction of sterility between species is still

---

[80] Here Romanes repeated his main criticism of Darwin's theory. [RAM]

[81] At p. 348 Romanes had not referred to "prolonged exposure to similar conditions of life, and prevention of intercrossing by geographical barriers, or by migration". [RAM]

left unexplained. This it is that my theory of physiological selection seeks to explain[82]. And the theory consists merely in pointing to the fact that wherever, among all the possible variations of the highly variable reproductive system, there arises towards any parent form any degree of sterility which does not extend to the varietal form, there a new species must necessarily take its origin. For, even though the varietal form continues to live on the same area as its parent form, intercrossing is prevented by the primary distinction of sterility, with the consequence of secondary distinctions subsequently arising by way of independent variability – just as happens when the barrier to intercrossing, instead of being physiological, is geographical.

It makes no essential difference to my theory whether the causes of this particular variation on the part of the reproductive system are extrinsic or intrinsic; nor does it make any difference whether the variation first occurs in a high or in a low degree. [p. 399] But many reasons have been given to show that most probably, in a large majority of cases, the primary distinction has likewise been the primordial distinction, and thus became the condition to the subsequent appearance of secondary distinctions by independent variability.

Moreover, one very important reason was given to show that, in all probability, the primary distinction is not only a *condition* to the subsequent appearance of secondary distinctions, but itself the *cause* of them; for Mr. Darwin has shown that when the reproductive system undergoes any variation, the consequences to progeny are apt to consist in variations affecting other parts of the organism. So that the prevention of intercrossing by physiological barriers differs from such prevention by geographical barriers, or by migration, in that, over and above the influence of independent variability, there is a direct causal connection between the agency which prevents intercrossing and the subsequent production of secondary specific characters.

Nevertheless, reasons have also been given to show that, in a small minority of cases, this historical order may have been reversed – the primary distinction having been superinduced by the secondary, as we sometimes (though very rarely) find to have been the case with our

---

[82] Romanes assumes that some degree of sterility produces new species – and, therefore, species will be mutually sterile. However, his theory would be unable to explain the mutual sterility of species produced under geographical isolation. [RAM]

domesticated varieties, but which we usually find to have been the case with genera, &c. Even, however, where such has been the case with natural varieties living on the same area, it is the principles of physiological selection that have determined the result; for it can only have been those secondary distinctions which happened to have been able to induce the primary distinction that were, for this reason, allowed to survive. Thus in all cases where the evolution of species has not been due to the prevention of intercrossing by geographical barriers or by migration, it has probably been due to such prevention by the principles of physiological selection. Or, otherwise stated, all specific types which now display any degree of sterility towards allied types, are probably so many records of the particular variation with which we are concerned having arisen in the reproductive systems of their ancestry. For, not only has it been shown, on antecedent grounds, that the occurrence of this particular variation is in the highest degree probable, but it has also been shown that, as a matter of actual observation, it does occur in individuals, in varieties, and in species. Indeed, as regards species, the argument here resolved itself into a mere [p. 400] statement of fact, namely, that all natural varieties which have not been otherwise prevented from intercrossing, and which have been allowed to survive long enough to develop any differences worth mentioning, are now found to be protected from intercrossing by the bar of sterility – that is, by a previous change or variation in the reproductive system of the kind which my theory requires. In many cases, no doubt, this particular change, or variation, has been caused by the season of flowering or of pairing having been either advanced or retarded in a section of a species, or to sundry other influences of an extrinsic kind; but probably in a still greater number of cases it has been due to what I have called intrinsic causes, or to the "spontaneous" variability of the reproductive system itself. In order to show how large a part the principles thus explained have probably played in the evolution of species, many arguments, which it would be tedious again to enumerate, have been drawn from the inutility of so large a proportion of secondary specific distinctions, from the swamping effects of intercrossing in the absence of physiological barriers, from the multiplication of species, and from the leading or most general facts of geographical distribution. Lastly, the relations between natural and physiological selection have been shown to be co-operative, the latter allowing the former to act by interposing its laws of sterility, with the result that secondary specific distinctions may be either adaptive or non-adaptive in character. On the other hand, natural selection may assist physiological selection by setting a premium both on the primary and on the secondary distinctions – *i. e.* encouraging the work both of sterilizing species and of diversifying their characters.

In conclusion, therefore, it seems to me almost impossible to doubt, when so many large and general facts combine in pointing to the principles of physiological selection, that these principles must be accredited with a highly important share in the evolution of species. Mr. Darwin has well said, "From the laws governing the various grades of sterility being so uniform throughout the animal and vegetable kingdoms, we may infer that the cause, whatever it may be, is the same, or nearly the same, in all cases." This cause, as he candidly shows in the paragraphs from which the quotation is made[*], obviously cannot have been natural selection. But to my mind it appears no less obvious that the [p. 401] cause in question is the cause which I have termed physiological selection[83]. For what are the effects which stand to be explained? Broadly stated, these effects are simply millions and millions of cases where there is a constant association between secondary specific characters, whether useful or unuseful, and the primary specific characters of sterility with allied forms. Be it observed that all these innumerable cases are alike in *kind*, however much they may differ in regard to the *degree* of sterility. In a considerable proportion of cases there is no sterility at all, and from this zero level we encounter all degrees of it, until we reach the maximum degree, where sterility is absolute.

Now, we have seen that these differences are exactly what my theory requires. For, 1st, in a considerable proportion of cases intercrossing has been prevented by geographical barriers and by migration; in these cases, therefore, physiological selection has had nothing to do with the evolution of species, which thus continue, as we might have expected, fertile *inter se*. 2nd, in many other cases physiological selection must have been assisted in its work of preventing intercrossing, whether by partial barriers of a geographical

---

[*] 'Origin of Species,' ed. 6, p. 248.

[83] As was already remarked above, the theory of physiological selection would be unable to explain the mutual sterility of species produced by geographical isolation; but he *denied* that species produced by geographical isolation were mutually infertile. [RAM]

kind, partial migrations, slight changes of climate, habitat, instinct, and so forth; in these cases, therefore, the resulting species now continue to manifest corresponding fertility between themselves, or fertility in all degrees. Hence, if sterility between allied species were always absolute, or even always considerable, the fact would be fatal to my theory; for this would show that sterility between allied forms must have been due to some cause other than the mere, but necessary, preservation of one particular kind of variation, whenever it happens to arise. But, as matters actually stand, we are able to explain the absence of sterility by the absence of physiological selection, and the presence of different degrees of sterility by the presence of different degrees of such selection.

Confining, then, our attention to that large proportional number of cases where the association in question obtains, and disregarding the different degrees of sterility, what really stands to be explained is the great and general fact of the association itself. For what does this fact imply? It implies that (the now explained exceptions apart), so soon as natural varieties become entitled to take rank as species, they are found to be varieties which, however much they may differ in other or secondary [p. 402] distinctions, agree in presenting the constant distinction in respect of their reproductive systems. In other words, systematists, in their classification of species, have always been engaged in unconsciously tabulating the records of cases where overwhelming intercrossing with parent forms has been prevented; and the only way in which we can account for the now very frequent occurrence of sterility between allied species is by supposing that in these cases it was this sterility which prevented the intercrossing, or constituted the condition to these species being formed. It serves still further to enforce this view of the case when we try to imagine what would happen if the now existing sterility between all allied species, which present it, were suddenly removed. In this case free intercrossing within the limits of each genus would soon reduce all specific types living on common areas to as small a number of species as there are now genera. But if this is what would certainly be the result on all common areas if the physiological conditions now existing were removed, must we not conclude that it was owing to the fact of these conditions that the now existing species arose?

Or, again, let us contrast the difference between natural species and domesticated varieties. These, as we have seen, resemble each other in every respect save in the one respect of mutual sterility. Can we, therefore, doubt that this condition, so often as it occurs, has played the same part in the evolution of natural species as the prevention of intercrossing by artificial barriers has played in the evolution of domesticated varieties? Or can we doubt that if intercrossing were in any other way prevented, natural species would resemble domesticated varieties still more closely in presenting well-marked differences of type without this peculiar association with the barrier of sterility? But if any one should doubt this, we have only to point to the unquestionable fact, that where intercrossing has been otherwise prevented – whether by geographical barriers or by migration – such well-marked differences of type have arisen, though in these cases they are not necessarily associated with the physiological barrier in question. Therefore, when this barrier is present, how can it be reasonable to doubt that its connection with the other differences of type is a connection of causality? For does not this extraordinarily general connection prove that it is only those cases of variation in any other part of any organism which happen to have been associated with the physiological barrier of sterility that have [p. 403] been able to survive under all circumstances where they would have otherwise inevitably perished by free intercrossing?

Looking to the very general association on which I am dwelling, I cannot wonder that in the pre-Darwinian days naturalists were led to suppose that the primary distinction of sterility was divinely-accorded to species, for the purpose of preventing their secondary distinctions from becoming lost by intercrossing. And I cannot help feeling that these naturalists were less blind than their successors; for at least they had an intelligible theory whereby to explain the general association which we are considering, whereas their successors have absolutely no theory at all. They are, therefore, much in the same position as a man might be who wonders at the constant association between a flowing river and a continuously descending excavation; for in both cases the association is much too frequent and general to be accounted for by chance, so that, if it is not to be accounted for by design, there only remains the alternative of accounting for it by a connection of causality. Yet, naturalists are now in the same state of mind as the man above supposed; they merely wonder at the association without perceiving its obvious import. For, assuredly, it is quite as obvious that species could not exist as species without the physiological condition of sterility, as it is that a river could not exist as a river without the physical condition of declivity. And just as in the latter case, wherever the requisite physical conditions occur, streams and rivers come into existence by way of natural consequence, so in the former case, wherever the requisite physiological conditions occur, species and genera arise as a no less inevitable result.

It only remains to be said that the theory of physiological selection has this immense advantage over every other theory that has ever been propounded on the origin of species: it admits of being either demonstrated or destroyed by verification [84]. But the process of verification will be a most laborious one, and cannot be satisfactorily completed (even if many naturalists should engage upon it) without the expenditure of years of methodical research. In view of this consideration, I have deemed it best to publish my theory before undertaking the labour of verification; for, by so doing, I hope to induce other naturalists to cooperate with me in carrying on the research in different parts of the world. With this object, I will conclude by briefly [p. 404] sketching out the lines on which the work of verification may proceed.

There are two main branches of testing inquiry, the one experimental, and the other systematic. It is open to the systematist, in any department either of botany or zoology, to utilize his knowledge as a specialist in the following way. Let him cast about for closely allied species which are thoroughly well separated from one another, either by geographical barriers or by migration. When he has found any two closely allied species which, for either of these reasons, he feels justified in certainly concluding can never have had an opportunity of intercrossing, let him ascertain whether they are not fertile with one another[85]. The species ought to be as closely allied as possible, because, if they differ in any considerable degree, even though the distinction between them is nominally specific, it really approaches a distinction that is generic; and in the case of genera there is no question as to sterility being due to a general difference of organic type. Moreover, the specialist ought not to rest satisfied with

---

[84] In the remaining part of his paper, Romanes describes how his theory could be tested. His epistemological approach is naïve, since he believes that a theory could be *proved* (demonstrated) by verification. However, the proposal of explicit tests of the theory is valuable. [RAM]

[85] According to Romanes' theory, closely related species produced by geographical isolation should remain mutually fertile. [RAM]

only a few observations. His aim ought rather to be to make his observations over a large number of species, tabulate the results, and then see whether the average amount of sterility yielded by all his selected species is not considerably lower than a similar average obtained by selecting a similar number of closely allied species now inhabiting the same continuous area – taking care, however, to choose areas which are believed to have been continuous for long periods of time. Perhaps the best rule to follow (especially in the case of plants) would be to take species which are peculiar to oceanic islands, and to match these with allied species on mainlands, for the first set of tables; while, for the second set, allied species, both of which are peculiar to the same large continental area, should be chosen[86]. If these observations were made over a considerable number of cases, I should expect them to show an unmistakable difference in the results of the two sets of averages. But it would be necessary to make them over a considerable number of cases, because by this method of inquiry we could never be sure that all modifying conditions had been excluded. Even if we could know the life-histories of each species chosen, there would still remain the element of doubt which is incidentally mentioned by Mr. Darwin in another connection – namely, that "if a species was rendered sterile with some one compatriot, sterility with other species would (?might) [p. 405] follow as a necessary contingency." So that, in view of these considerations, I am disposed to think that even wholly negative results yielded by this branch of inquiry would not be absolutely fatal to my theory, although, no doubt, most damaging to its probability.

The other branch of inquiry consists in looking out for cases of two well-marked natural varieties living together on the same area, and ascertaining by experiment whether these are not more fertile within their own limits, than they are with one another[87]. Plants would lend themselves to these experiments much more readily than animals; and in the case of plants the experiments would not be very difficult to try,

---

[86] In this case, according to Romanes, the only possible explanation of the production of new species would be physiological selection; therefore, in this case, a considerable degree of mutual sterility should be observed. [RAM]

[87] Of course, any well marked natural varieties living together on the same area *must* have some degree of mutual sterility, otherwise they would not remain distinct. The experimental confirmation of this situation does not confirm that the difference between those natural varieties was *produced* by physiological selection. [RAM]

while the results when obtained would be less open to doubt than those obtainable by the method above mentioned. I therefore hope that botanists in different parts of the world will deem it worth their while to see whether it is not possible to gain this direct evidence, at once of evolution as a fact, and of physiological selection as a method.

The points to be attended to in conducting these experiments are as follows. Let the varieties be well marked, or, at least, constant within themselves; let there be no question that both the varieties are endemic as well as common to the area which they occupy. In conducting the experiments care should be taken not to disturb the natural conditions of the individuals chosen, whether by transplantation or in any other way. And, of course, it is needless to add that not only care must be taken, but certainty secured, that the only source of fertilization of the individuals chosen is that of the pollen used by the observer. The experiments which ought to be conducted over a large number of individuals, will in every case divide themselves into four sets: – 1st, fertilization of A by B; 2nd, fertilization of B by A; 3rd, of A by A; and 4th, of B by B; where A and B are the two varieties in question. In every one experiment of these four sets of experiments the seed which is yielded must be counted and sown. When all the experiments are over, let it thus be ascertained whether there is any difference in the *degrees* of fertility which have been yielded by experiments 1 and 2, and by 3 and 4 respectively. [p. 406]

Postscript

In the discussion which followed the reading of this paper[88], certain difficulties or objections were put forward by one or two of the more eminent naturalists who happened to be present. These I answered verbally; but, inasmuch as they may also occur to readers of the paper, I will here briefly consider those among them which do not appear to have been sufficiently anticipated in the course of the preceding pages.

First, it was objected that breeding in and in has a tendency to deteriorate offspring, and therefore that physiological selection, by limiting the area of breeding, would yield a variety less able than its

---

[88] This refers to the discussion after the presentation of Romanes' paper at the Linnean Society. [RAM]

parent form to compete successfully in the struggle for existence. This objection, however, would only be of any force where an exceedingly small number of individuals are concerned[89]; and even then, I think, it may be neglected, seeing that in the course of a very few generations consanguinity becomes diluted in so rapid a ratio, even in the case of species which produce but few at a birth. On this point I may refer to the 'Origin of Species,' pp. 72, 238, and 252, to show that even Mr. Darwin (who more than any other writer has insisted on the benefit arising from cross-fertilization) disregards the effect of interbreeding, where more than a very few individuals are concerned.

Next, it was objected that it could be of no *use* to a varietal type that it should be separated from the parental. I have, however, argued that the use would be three-fold: 1st, the variety would thus be started on an independent course of history; 2nd, it would therefore be able "to seize on many and widely diversified places in the economy of nature;"[90] and, 3rd, it would derive the advantage that breeders find in keeping their strains from intercrossing. But, over and above all this, the theory of physiological selection does not require that the separation in question should be of any use; and, therefore, this objection to the theory falls to the ground as irrelevant. So long as there is no actual *detriment* arising to the variety on account of its being separated from the parent, any ideas derived from the theory of natural selection are plainly without hearing upon the subject.

Lastly, it was in effect suggested that the theory of physiological selection is merely the restatement of a fact. For, [p. 407] as I have myself argued (pp. 361, 399-400),[91] upon the general theory of evolution it must be accepted as a fact that, so soon as varieties have diverged from their parental type sufficiently far to take rank as

---

[89] The objection seems really relevant, because the rise of a large number of individuals with exactly the same random reproductive variation, in the same area, at the same time, would be unlikely. Donald Forskyke claims that Romanes did introduce the idea of collective variation (FORSDYKE, Donald R. George Romanes, William Bateson, and Darwin's 'weak point'. *Notes and Records of the Royal Society*, **64**: 139-154, 2010, at p. 142). Indeed, he did so, a few years later – but even then, he provided no evidence that the required kind of collective variation was possible or real. [RAM]

[90] This seems unsound. If the initial difference is only a reproductive one, this would imply no way of profiting from diversified pales in the economy of nature. [RAM]

[91] All pages pointed out by Romanes refer to the original page numbers of this article. [RAM]

species, some such change in the reproductive system as that of sterility with allied forms has usually been found to have occurred. Now, it is perfectly true that this is the well-known fact, and, moreover, as I have previously endeavoured to insist, that it is the fact which more than any other stands to be explained by any theory of the origin of species. But, obviously, the theory of physiological selection is something more than a mere re-statement of this fact: it is an *explanation* of the fact in terms of evolutionary philosophy.

First, let it be observed that the supposed objection is not concerned with any question touching the validity of the evidence adduced to show that the particular kind of variation on which my theory depends does actually take place; nor is the objection concerned with any doubt as to the extent in which this variation may have operated in the origination of species. On the contrary, the objection goes upon the ground of accepting all the evidence which I have adduced upon these points, and then representing that, granting it all, it merely amounts to a re-statement of fact. Well, let the evidence be granted, and, therefore, let it be assumed that the majority of natural species are so many records of a particular kind of variation having taken place in the reproductive systems of ancestors. The issue then resolves itself into the question whether this is a mere re-statement of fact, or whether it serves to throw any new light in the way of explanation.

By an explanation I understand the pointing out of effects as due to the operation of causes. In the present instance, the effect which has to be explained is the differentiation of specific types. This I have sought to do by invoking the agency of a well-known event – viz., that of variation –and showing that whenever this cause affects the reproductive system in a particular way, a new species must arise as an effect. Now, I believe that this mode of viewing the problem as to the origin of species is not only new, but, if true, serves to solve the problem, or to explain the facts. The facts, indeed, were there before, as must always be the case before an explanation can be suggested; but an explanation consists in placing the facts in a certain relation to one another – i. e. in a relation of proved causality. In the present instance [p. 408] this, so far as I am aware, has not been previously done. The facts of variation have been known, and the facts of specific sterility have been known; but hitherto it has not been suggested that the former may stand to the latter in the relation of cause to effect, or that when a particular kind of variation occurs in the reproductive system a new species must necessarily ensue. The very general association between mutual sterility and specific differences of other kinds has, indeed, forced itself upon the attention of naturalists; but naturalists have attempted to explain the association by this, that, and the other collateral cause, such as divine interposition, uniform conditions of life, and so forth. The present theory, on the other hand, seeks to explain this association as itself an association of cause and effect; the theory regards a species as nothing more than a variety, where the variation happens to have affected the reproductive system in a particular way – thus leading to physiological separation, and so eventually to other morphological changes, as previously argued. Now, whatever may be thought as to the probability of this explanation, to me it appears evident that it is an explanation, and not merely a restatement of fact. For, if not, where has been the need of all that has been written for the purpose of endeavouring to explain the association? If it has ever before been recognized that species are the effects of variations in the reproductive systems of ancestry, I cannot understand why this should not have been clearly stated; and still less can I understand why, with so simple an explanation before the mind, any naturalist should have cast about for other causes of a collateral kind. What I can understand is that more evidence should be demanded of the truth of the present explanation; but this is not the point with which the objection before us is concerned.

The real standing of the matter is simply this. Evolutionists have hitherto regarded mutual sterility as one among the effects of specific differentiation, and they have therefore been led to seek for causes which might be held adequate to account for this effect. My theory, on the other hand, regards the sterility, wherever it occurs, as itself the cause of specific differentiation; and this whether the sterility be spontaneous or induced by changes going on in other parts of the organism, as previously explained. Evolutionists have hitherto failed to find the causes of which they have been in search; and, according to my view, necessarily so, inasmuch as there are no such causes to be found. [p. 409] The association between specific divergence and mutual sterility has therefore appeared, in a high decree, inexplicable; so that, in Mr. Darwin's words, "the real difficulty" presented to evolutionists has been to explain why mutual sterility "has so generally occurred with natural varieties, as soon as they have been permanently modified in a sufficient degree to take rank as species" – a difficulty which he thought we were still far from solving, inasmuch as "We are far from precisely knowing the cause." But the whole of this apparently great and inexplicable difficulty has arisen on account of regarding the sterility, in some way or another, the *consequence* of a natural variety becoming "permanently modified." Once let the point of view be changed, or once let us see in the sterility the *antecedent* of the permanent modification, and, as it appears to me, there is an end of the matter: "the real difficulty" has vanished, seeing that we are no longer "far from precisely knowing the cause" of the general association between sterility and divergence. But, if so, can it be said that the solution of such a problem, the removal of such a difficulty, or the pointing out of such a causal relation, is nothing more than a re-statement of fact? Yet this is what the objection which I am considering amounts to; for, as previously remarked, it goes upon the ground of accepting my whole argument, and questions only the character of that argument as an explanation.

It may serve to place this matter in a still clearer light if I briefly indicate one important consequence of my suggested explanation of the origin of species, and one which certainly could not arise if this explanation were nothing more than a re-statement of facts already recognized. Hitherto it has been the aim, or argumentative bias, of evolutionists to disparage – and even to ignore – the swamping influence of intercrossing; for, according to the supposition that sterility of species is an effect of morphological divergence, it obviously follows that this swamping influence of intercrossing must be held inimical to such divergence, or to the formation of new species. According to my view, on the other hand, it is just this swamping influence of intercrossing that constitutes the *raison d'être* of all species which present any degree of sterility with allied forms. For, according to my view, it is only this one particular variation in the way of such sterility which, being in virtue of its own character shielded from the swamping influence, is for this reason allowed to survive: it is the one particular variation that is [p. 410] selected to constitute a new species. Intercrossing is thus regarded as standing in the same kind of relation to the genesis of species as the struggle for existence stands to that of adaptive structures: it is the destroying tendency which furnishes the needful condition to a selective process: it is the agency which obliterates all other variations, save those of a particular kind . Therefore, according to my theory of the origin of species, the greater the swamping influence of intercrossing the better must be the conditions for evolving species mutually sterile with one another; while, as we have seen, precisely the opposite consequence follows from all previous theories upon this subject.

Probably more than enough has now been said to dispose of the criticism which I am considering, or to show that the theory of physiological selection offers a real explanation of the origin of species[92], and does so by going to work at the very root of the problem. I will therefore only add that the real idea in the minds of those who advanced this criticism must, it appears to me, have been that my suggested explanation of the origin of species opens up another and a more ultimate problem – namely, granting that species have originated in the way supposed, what have been the causes of the particular kind of variation in the reproductive system which the theory requires? This, of course, is a perfectly intelligible question, and one that must immediately suggest itself to the mind: my failure to meet it is therefore apt to give rise to the impression that my theory is imperfect. But, as briefly stated in the paper itself, this question is really not one with which the theory of physiological selection can properly be regarded as having anything to do. This theory has only to take the facts of variation in general as granted, and then to construct out of them its suggested explanation of the origin of species. No doubt it would be most interesting to discover the causes of every variation that constitutes the beginning of a new specific character; but our inability to do this does not invalidate the theory of physiological selection, any more than it does the theory of natural selection. Objections, indeed, have been raised against the theory of natural selection on this very ground – namely, that it does not explain the causes of those variations on the occurrence of which it depends. But these objections are clearly illogical. It constitutes no part of the theory of natural selection to explain these variations; this is a problem which belongs to the future of physiology, and no doubt we shall have long to wait before we derive much light upon it. But it is enough for the explanation which is furnished by Mr. Darwin's theory of the evolution of adaptive structures by natural selection, that the variations in question take place; and similarly as to the present theory of the evolution of species by physiological selection.

Whatever, therefore, may be thought as to the truth of this theory, or as to the extent of its applicability, it is certainly something very

---

[92] The wording of this sentence implies that Romanes did not believe that the theory of physiological selection was *likely* or *probable*, but that it was *true*. [RAM]

much more than a bare re-statement of fact. If the evidence which I have presented on these points is accepted (as it must be by the criticism with which I am dealing), the explanatory value of the theory may be estimated by the consideration that what Mr. Darwin has called the "mystery of mysteries"[†] ceases to be mysterious in any other sense or degree than the general fact that offspring do not always and in every respect resemble their parents. The birth of a new species becomes, for instance, less mysterious than the birth of a child with six toes, inasmuch as the variation which it implies is one of less departure from the specific type. Nay, it becomes even less mysterious than the occurrence of what I have termed individual incompatibility – a variation which, on account of its apparently trivial character, Mr. Darwin apologizes for so much as mentioning. Hence, unless it be denied that the clearing up of a mystery constitutes an explanation, the present theory is unquestionably an explanation of the only phenomena with which it is concerned. Although it makes no attempt at explaining the physiological causes which underlie the phenomena of variation in general, if the evidence which has been given be accepted, the theory does furnish a real explanation of the origin of species, by proving that there is one particular variation which, so often as it has taken place, must necessarily have constituted the originating cause of a new specific form.

[†] Viz. – the problem of the origin of species, which, as shown in the preceding paper, his theory of natural selection serves only in small part to explain.

Printed in Great Britain
by Amazon